MILLENNIALS' GUIDE TO
DIVERSITY, EQUITY & INCLUSION

What No One Ever Told You About The
Importance of Diversity, Equity, and Inclusion

D1264584

LISA D. JENKINS
JENNIFER P. WISDOM

Published by Winding Pathway Books

WINDING PATHWAY BOOKS

ISBN (print): 978-1-954374-03-4
ISBN (e-book): 978-1-954374-02-7

Book design by Nick Caya at Word-2-Kindle
Cover design by Alexandrea Merlo and Diego G. Diaz
Photo Credit: Diego G. Diaz

For more information or bulk orders, visit www.leadwithwisdom.com

Printed in the United States of America

Advance Praise for *Millennials' Guide to Diversity, Equity & Inclusion*

"The *Millennial's Guide to Diversity, Equity & Inclusion* is a great read, full of amazing content. Each chapter asks thought-provoking questions, helping the reader think more deeply about their identity and the impact culture has on how we see ourselves and the world around us. The authors challenge us to own our bias and be mindful of how bias shapes our engagements. Do you want a crash course on diversity, equity, and inclusion? If the answer is yes, then pick up this book right now and start reading it. I can't wait to share this with some of my clients."

-Glen Guyton
Diversity, Equity, & Inclusion Consultant
GuyStar Enterprises, LLC

"*Millennial's Guide to Diversity, Equity & Inclusion* is an intelligent, thoughtful conversation starter and personal journey mate. As an educator, recognizing, understanding, and appreciating diversity, equity, and inclusion have been the forefront of my practice. As a Millennial, I found value in not only seeing myself through the eyes of the authors but also in acknowledging the importance of doing the continuous work to truly understand myself AND others -- an understanding that highlights differences in an "also" not "only" style. The topics were dual reasons and reminders that in these ever changing times, we all need course correction to serve as an inclusive compass leading us to live as our best selves; which ultimately will make the world a better place for everyone. "

-Amanda Marie Spivey, M. Ed.
Professional Educator

"For more than two decades, I have worked with thousands of Millennials at campuses nationwide. Millennials are known for their concern for social issues and advocacy to make the world a more equitable place. As diversity, equity, and inclusion has moved to the forefront of our consciousness, this comprehensive guide is the perfect solution to educate and empower millennials to make a difference. The *Millennials Guide to Diversity, Equity & Inclusion* serves as an essential guide to heighten their understanding and empowerment to create an equitable and just world. Everyone should read this!"

-Elaine Pasqua, CSP
Certified Speaking Professional and President
Pasqua Productions, Inc.

"I enjoyed the opportunity to read the *Millennials' Guide to Diversity, Equity & Inclusion*. As a Millennial and DEI expert, I found the book to be very insightful and full of a-ha! moments. I loved every chapter, as each chapter provided a deeper understanding of self, culture, and stereotypes, as well as diversity, equity, and inclusion. The book highlighted so many aspects of today's world! *Millennials' Guide to Diversity, Equity & Inclusion is* relevant, relatable, and timely."

-Tonia Morris
Founder & CEO
Simply HR Inc.

"*Millennials' Guide to Diversity, Equity & Inclusion* is an amazingly helpful guide to understand diversity, inclusion, race, gender, and social practices that affect people living within today's society. It will help those who read it develop sensitivity, awareness, and a strong understanding of people from varied socio-cultural experiences, which, in turn, can assist in developing a more peaceful and gentle society."

-Rev. Kelly U. Farrow, Ph.D.

"Before becoming the leader of an organization, as a Millennial growing my career, I had to learn about the power of bringing my whole self to work the hard way. Learning how important, and special, it is to do this took a lot of trial and error. *Millennials' Guide to Diversity, Equity & Inclusion* book provides a solid plan and advice to figure out how to approach your career in a way that lifts you AND your organization up without sacrificing your integrity."

-Thomas Chernick
Director, New York Chapter of the National Gay and Lesbian Chamber of Commerce

"As a community development executive who has led nonprofit organizations and government agencies, I know that it has been my Millennial colleagues who have the burning desire to foster positive social change. I am pleased to provide them the space and support to do so. I am thrilled that I now can also arm them with this how-to manual to guide them through their leadership journeys as they get into - as the late Civil Rights Movement activist and Congressman John Lewis called it - good trouble."

-Taneshia Nash Laird
President & CEO
Newark Symphony Hall

"*Millennials' Guide to Diversity, Equity & Inclusion* is a must read for both established professionals and emerging leaders alike. The authors' scholarly -- yet practical -- approach leads readers through the much needed process of self-reflection and empowers with tools and techniques to navigate real world situations. This will be an instant addition to the York Early College Academy Library!

-Reginald Madden
Academic Affairs Manager
Liaison to York Early College Academy

Millennials' Guide to Diversity, Equity & Inclusion is NOT just for Millennials. This book is the single most effective guide to success in the "real world," -- to changing the real world for the better -- that I have seen. It's short, to the point, thorough, and chock-full of wisdom. Diversity, equity, and inclusion are the topic, but life, success, and fairness are the goals this book leads you to. This is MUST READING for everyone in the public sphere: clergy, business, political, education leaders – all will find this guide invaluable for navigating the post-Covid world.

Rabbi Burton L. Visotzky, PhD
Director, Milstein Center for Interreligious Dialogue
Jewish Theological Seminary

Table of Contents

Foreword

In the light of racial injustice being on the world stage, the question that many of us ask ourselves is "What is my role in changing the world to reduce racial injustice?"

Unbeknownst to me, many factors and influences have shaped how I view the world. I did not have the wherewithal to understand this for years. Once I realized that I am in charge of my views on the world, however, I set out to curate my own existence, views, and experiences and shape my own opinions of the world around me. The first step for many of you is to open your eyes to your ownership of how you move through the world. The next step is accessing resources, exposure and experiences that will open your eyes to this world that you may not see right now.

Millennials' Guide to Diversity, Equity & Inclusion can help you with that next step.

In college, we watched movie after movie and read book after book that catalogued the experiences of black and brown bodies colonized by white bodies. We discussed the pervasive impact colonization still has on black and brown people throughout the diaspora. I remember leaving class crying (more than once), calling my mother and saying, "This is what happened! This is what I learned about! What do I do about it? It can't stay this way! How can I change it?" My mother's guidance was always, "Takiyah, you do what you can, with what you have, when you can." You, too, can understand the wider context and impact that injustice, discrimination, prejudice, oppression, and exclusion have had and continue to have on all of our communities and cultures.

Millennials' Guide to Diversity, Equity & Inclusion can help you with that next step.

At Google, I partner with CapitalG, Google's late stage investment group, to support 40+ hyper-growth stage companies in their efforts to diversify, include, and create equitable spaces and practices. Many of these organizations have little to no Diversity, Equity, and Inclusion (DEI) infrastructure. But they simply cannot ignore the need for it now. More organizations are understanding the importance of DEI, and you can help. People drive an organization. Without people working together, feeling included, feeling like they belong, feeling like they can grow and develop, feeling like they have access to the same opportunities, companies fail to reach their higher potential.

In helping these organizations build out models for DEI, I learned that many do not have the appropriate resources to even get started or even know where to start. I established a working group to help them get the knowledge, resources, and support to begin to understand their role in DEI. The working group brought together the diversity leaders across the 40 companies to share their experiences and where their respective organization was on its DEI journey. We exposed them to leaders within Google who had been working on these efforts for years, and who created and led successful DEI programs, and who put Google on the right track to be a more conscientious workspace. We kept developing DEI-focused acumen, closing the gaps on DEI experience, knowledge, information, and resources. The acts felt small, but they were powerful to these individuals and impactful to their organizations. You can look at those small acts, too, closing gaps in knowledge and experiences in your organization, your church, your team, your family, your community.

Millennials' Guide to Diversity, Equity & Inclusion can help you with that next step.

As you read this book, and particularly as you come to *Part 5. How to Change the World*, I encourage you to keep in mind that changing the world is relative. Changing the world doesn't necessarily mean impacting 7 billion lives at once. It doesn't mean single-handedly ending all injustices forever. It does mean impacting the world around you. It means that as a leader you are actively seeking out opportunities to increase diversity in your workforce. It means challenging the status quo when it oppresses and represses others. It means increasing inclusion. It means ensuring each contributor in your work environment has a sense of belonging and has a sense of purpose within your team and organization.

So now that you have *Millennials' Guide to Diversity, Equity & Inclusion*: Do the work. Change the world by changing *your* world. Change the world by making someone else's life better. You are powerful enough and capable enough to take the steps and close the gaps. You can impact significant changes in your organization.

Do what you can, with what you have, when you can. You will start to see change. And you will know that you had taken action when it was important.

- Takiyah Johnson
Women in Tech at Google, Inc.

Introduction

Diversity, equity, and inclusion have moved to the forefront of national discourse in the U.S. and around the world. As consultants and educators, many Millennials have shared with us they are aware of this unique opportunity in time to address diversity and would like to be part of the solution. We also hear from Millennials who feel that the enormous historical and social issues around race, gender, and power are overwhelming and that they feel they have nothing to offer to the conversation about diversity. Finally, heated conversations have become the norm, so it adds another level of complication to an already challenging set of issues.

We wrote this book to speak directly to Millennials about diversity, equity, and inclusion. We aim to strengthen your resolve and to help you understand that not only are you a change agent, but that positive change can begin with *you*. Actually, change *must* begin with you. There is too much at stake for good people who want to make progress stay on the sidelines due to confusion, overwhelm, or helplessness.

In this book, we start in *Part 1. Understanding Yourself*, by providing opportunities for you to learn about yourself. Who are you? Who are your people? How do you define yourself, and what do you value? If you only work through one section of the book, it's this one. Yes, it's *work*. Work to understand yourself and your history, conflicts that informed your ancestry and development, and how the many different aspects of who you are and what you believe shape how you interact with the world. How you see others, and how you are seen. This is critical – and rewarding – work.

In *Part 2. Understanding Diversity*, we walk readers through some basics of diversity, equity, and inclusion. We start with definitions and describe both how these concepts emerged, their historical relevance, and why they raise such complex feelings today.

1

Part 3. Understanding Others helps individuals of all backgrounds and experiences understand more about people who are different from them. Any one of these chapters is merely a very basic summary of issues; any one of them has been a lifetime of study for many scholars. To that end, we provide a substantial list of further reading on each of these topics.

In *Part 4. Making Our Way in the World*, we discuss some basics of how to use your new diversity-mindedness to interact with others every day. We include addressing mindfulness, perspective, allyship, and communication so that you can navigate everyday situations competently and respectfully.

Part 5. How to Change the World describes how you can pick up speed and become a force for good. This part is what you've been waiting for! In this chapter, we describe how to build belonging, build bridges, adapt to ongoing changes and become the diversity, equity, and inclusion superhero you want to be.

In our final section, *Part 6. Leading Diversity, Equity, and Inclusion*, we apply these recommendations to leaders in the workplace. When you are in charge of teams, you have a unique position of authority to change the world with even more impact. As a leader, emerging leader, or aspiring leader, check out this section to boost your positive impact. The book concludes with an extensive reading list and glossary.

We want to be very clear with you -- it will be a lot of work to read through and contemplate the issues discussed in this book, addressing challenges that emerged over hundreds of years and around the world related to diversity, equity, and inclusion. We promise you, though, this process will be worth it. And not to scare you, but this book is merely a beginning. This book is far from exhaustive on diversity, equity, and inclusion. Consider it a primer to get you started. Addressing diversity, equity, and inclusion is a lifetime experience toward understanding yourself and understanding others.

Lisa D. Jenkins
Jennifer P. Wisdom
December 2020

How to Use this Book

If you've read other books in the *Millennials' Guides* series (*Millennials' Guide to Work, Millennials' Guide to Management and Leadership, Millennials' and Generation Z Guide to Voting, Millennials' Guide to Relationships,* or *Millennials' Guide to the Construction Trades),* you know how this works. *Millennials' Guides* are not books necessarily best read cover to cover. We encourage you to review the table of contents and identify a challenge you are currently having or recently experienced. Turn to those pages to start finding a solution!

Each chapter includes a brief description, several things to think about, and activities that you may want to try. Many times, you can feel improvement after trying one option. You'll see some information repeated across different chapters because they're likely to be helpful for many problems. For complex challenges, you may want to attempt several interventions at the same time.

It's important to have patience and give the solutions and considerations a little bit of time to work. Some ideas that you try won't solve the problem but will make it a little better or make you think differently about the issue -- that's still success! If you don't feel comfortable trying an activity, try something else. Some of the activities are very low risk, such as changing your expectations of other people. Others can appear more challenging, such as directly discussing a concern with a family member, friend, or colleague. Start with actions that feel like lower risk to you and work your way up to more challenging actions.

As you work through the book, you'll get better at understanding diversity, equity, and inclusion; reading situations; responding respectfully to people you work with; building positive and diverse networks; and applying solutions effectively. Observe, be patient, clarify your own boundaries, and learn. The more you know what you want, the more you'll be able to achieve your goals. If you're not sure what you want, that's okay too--that's a perfect place to be while you're in your 20s and 30s. The goal of the strategies in this book is to help you develop skills that will serve you well as you continue to move forward in your lifelong exploration of diversity, equity, and inclusion.

Each of you reading this book is a unique person with talents to share with the world. Our hope is that this book can make it easier for you to do so. Good luck improving the world!

Part 1.
Understanding Yourself

Chapter 1.
Who Am I?

You may think that you have no control over the culture in your world or at the organization where you work. Not so! Not only do you impact your culture, but it is important to remember that you are a *part* of the culture in your world -- a very important part! *Who you are* shapes the culture around you. But first things first: do you know who you are?

1. **Often individuals, especially young people, feel that they have little to no say in the structure, environment and overall character of their world** or the organization for which they work. Know that your voice is important and you *can* impact the culture of your organization. Knowing who you are, and how you show up in multiple roles in different groups, can increase your impact in the world.

2. **Everyone has multiple aspects of their identity.** Identities may include ethnic, racial, national, gender, regional, sexual, personal, and organizational identities. These identities act in concert with one another, making you unique. Some parts of your identity you were born with (nationality, ethnicity). Others may change over time (group membership, religion, political affiliation). Who you are today is a result of countless interactions over time in which you discover who you are and how you fit into the world. What are some of your identities? These may be as a son or daughter, Puerto Rican, lesbian, child of immigrants, Muslim, New Yorker, or many more. Write down your current identities.

3. **Within the world, you are part of a larger group.** In fact, you're part of several larger groups. You are a part of your family, your community, social organizations, political clubs, professional organizations, religious groups, a generation, and

more. Even sports teams and social media groups count. And of course, your workplace. Write down a list of the various groups or organizations to which you belong, starting with your family.

4. **For the identities that you weren't born into, you have various ways of identifying how you fit into other groups.** These can include considering how you became a part of the groups you now affiliate with, increasing our awareness about the nature and history of those affiliations and identities, understanding rituals or rites of passage associated with these groups, attending events with others in this identity to build affiliation, and more. How you become affiliated with these groups can vary widely, from completing a membership form to apply to an organization, attending a ceremony or ritual and sticking with it, or a more formal initiation ceremony.

5. **Because society changes, along with the groups which make up our society, identities change as well.** Thinking back to when you were a child, how has your identity changed over the years? Have various parts of your identity become more important or less important over time? Are there parts of your identity that you would like to be more prominent or less prominent?

6. **Each of the groups you listed has its own values, norms and expectations,** which can be written, but more often, are unwritten. They're simply "known" – or in many cases, they are assumed to be known by all. Pick one of the groups that you belong to, and identify any values, norms, and expectations that may be written down. Then consider what values, norms, and expectations you believe the group shares that are not written down. Note these may be different from the written ones. These can include how the group determines its membership, how people treat outsiders, how members treat each other, how decisions are made, and more. Once you have a good list, share the list with a trusted other member of the group and see if you are in agreement.

7. **Once you have a sense of the values, norms, and expectations of a group,** identify whether you agree with them. Are they applied consistently and fairly to all members? What happens when members have different behavior or attitudes that conflict with the values, norms, and expectations in place? Do you think that the members of these groups are open to new ideas? Why or why not?

8. **How a group treats outsiders is an often-overlooked indicator of the group's values.** Often members within a group feel comfortable with one another so they feel that they can make remarks about outsiders that may seem harmless. Ethnic jokes, jokes about women or jokes about LGBTQ individuals might not seem like a big deal, but they are really the first level of prejudice. Have you ever heard others in any of your groups make such remarks? If so, how might that change the values, norms, and expectations you wrote down above? *Antilocution,* or hate speech (which includes jokes), lays the breeding ground for discriminatory practices and racism. If you've heard such comments before, how did others respond? How would you handle the situation if you heard someone in one or more of your groups using disparaging remarks or jokes about outsiders?

9. **Once you've written down this information,** hold on to it. We'll return to it later in the book. Feel free to update it as you need to, and to discuss it with others. And congratulations -- you've made a huge step forward in understanding who you are and how you fit in the world!

See also: **Chapter 2:** What is My Culture?

                         Chapter 4: What are My Values?

                         Chapter 5: How do I Define Myself?

Chapter 2.
What is My Culture?

Many people think that culture has to do with ethnic foods or perhaps the clothing that they see others wearing. But culture is far more than material aspects such as food and clothing. This can be problematic when we box culture narrowly into material and tangible elements. So ... what is culture?

1. **There are many definitions for culture.** A good, solid definition is that culture is *socially learned and transmitted behavior*. Culture is *what we do*. Yes, it's what we wear and what we eat. But it's also what we value and what we believe. These values and beliefs impact what we think of ourselves and how we interact and treat others.

2. **Beliefs are the assumptions that we choose to make about the world in which we live; they are part of our culture or subculture.** These may be associated with our group membership. For example, most religions profess a belief that killing people is wrong. Some religions profess a belief that killing animals for food is also wrong. Some of our beliefs are consistent with what our groups believe; others may be different from what our groups profess. Write down some of the assumptions or beliefs you have about the world. These could be about basic rules we should follow, the value of people or things. In general, if you think, "People should ..." or "Certain people should ..." what follows is one of your assumptions. Write it down and come back to it when you think of more.

3. **As a result of assumptions and beliefs, we think and behave in various ways.** For example, if we believe that all people are generally good, we behave differently than if we believe

all people are generally bad. We must remember that our behaviors affect not only our own outcomes in life, but those around us—particularly those groups in which we belong to—including our families and our workplace.

4. **Remember that culture is *learned*.** It is not innate. As we are continually learning and therefore changing, our culture also changes. As others learn and grow, they also change the culture. This includes our culture as individuals and the culture in our particular settings. This learning is both formal and informal. How do you learn about culture?

5. **There are several methods in which culture is transmitted to us.** We learn about our culture through methods such as those below. When you look at the assumptions and values you wrote down, how did you learn about them?

    a. *Direct instruction.* This is when we are directly taught what to believe about our culture. For example, many of us in the U.S. are taught in school colonists discovered the Americas (even though there were people living here already) and that Native Americans had primitive societies. This instruction reflects the values of the people teaching and may or may not be completely accurate.

    b. *Rewards and punishment.* When we do what we should be doing in our culture, we are often rewarded. Examples of these rewards are celebrations for achieving an educational accomplishment. Similarly, when we step out of line, we may be punished in some way, such as by disapproving looks, being ignored, or in some cases, physical punishment. Many times, people implement these rewards and punishment without really thinking about it; they're just repeating what they were taught.

    c. *Imitation and experimentation.* We often imitate people we admire, whether it's smoking because "cool kids" are smoking, wearing fancy clothes, or disliking the same people they dislike. Sometimes we experiment with who we want to resemble, so we try on those same behaviors and beliefs.

d. *Role playing.* Similar to imitation, we can try on roles. Many times, young children assume different roles when they are playing, such as parent/child, teacher/student, or cop/robber. This helps them figure out what people in those roles do by play-acting. As adults, we sometimes take on roles, such as leader, which allows us to try on different behaviors and views as well.

e. *Interaction.* Finally, interacting with others -- especially those different from us – helps us better understand our culture and their culture. There may be subtle differences, such as comfort with eye contact while speaking, or significant differences, like impropriety of speaking with someone of a different gender. The more we approach these interactions with an open mind and curiosity rather than judgment, the more we can learn about culture, both ours and others'.

6. **Although culture is transmitted using methods, agents are the conduits for those methods.** These agents may be authoritative, or personal to us, or not related to us at all. Agents include our family, school, peer groups, religion, workplace, and of course mass media. Consider the ways in which you were influenced by these different agents and how we all continue to be influenced by them. To look further into agents, go back to some of your group affiliations from Chapter 1. Consider what agents taught you values for those groups. If you're not sure, ask! For example, you could ask a parent or sibling about some of the beliefs instilled into you by your family. Or you could identify what messages you're receiving from mass media by watching television shows from the time when you were growing up. What were the lessons those shows displayed? Some lessons you might have picked up from television include: Hard work will/won't pay

off, life is/isn't fair, women and men make/don't make similar contributions to society. What are you finding?

7. **Remember your understanding of culture begins at birth and the transition continues throughout your lifetime.** It's an ongoing process! Be curious!

See also: **Chapter 1:** Who Am I?

Chapter 3: Who are My People?

Chapter 7: My Stereotypes

Chapter 3.
Who are My People?

How you approach the culture in your organization and in society is largely determined by your own understanding of culture and by your identity. The important thing to know about identity is that it is your self-definition. Your identity is self-defined by your distinct beliefs, attitudes, values and behaviors. Each of us is a product of our culture.

1. **Your culture is multifaceted.** This means that the various aspects of culture mentioned above and the degree to which they exist vary from person to person. When you think about all of the identities you have, what are the groups associated with these identities? Do you feel like you're a part of each of those groups? Do you relate? Do you feel these are your people?

2. **If there are groups that you do not affiliate with as "your people," think through why.** For example, someone who immigrated to the U.S. from Kenya as a teenager might or might not identify as "African American," even if it is technically accurate. Some people whose behaviors and feelings would indicate they are bisexual don't identify as part of the LGBTQ community – or may not even self-identify as bisexual! Are there any beliefs you have about groups or how those groups are perceived that make you not want to have them be your people?

3. **Studies show that more and more Americans are comfortable transitioning from one identity to another.** If you've changed any part of your identity (e.g., sexual orientation, profession, nationality, religion), how does that affect whether you affiliate with that group? Why do you

think this is the case? If you transition away from a group, there may be a process of grieving as you leave that part of your identity behind.

4. **Quite a few people attempt to mask their identity in order to fit in with dominant groups.** This is called "passing." The person is able to conceal their race, place of origin, or ethnicity, and publicly identifies as someone else. This could be for safety reasons or for other reasons. For example, some people who are LGBTQ "pass" as straight because many people assume heterosexuality, and it may be safer for them to let people assume they are straight. Are there any ways in which you actively or passively mask your identity? Do you know anyone who does this, and why they might? For most people, safety is paramount.

5. **Another practice that is used in the workplace is called code-switching.** This is when members of a particular group automatically adjust their language and vernacular to fit in with those in the mainstream or with another group to which they belong. Code-switching is not necessarily to hide one's identity. For many, it has become part of a natural behavior enabling the person to assimilate into the working environment. For example, many people temper their accents or slang when they are at work compared to when they are at home or with their peers. Do you do this in any way? Do you know people who do this?

6. **Be aware that seemingly equivalent aspects of "my people" may be different across different groups.** For example, many white people find aspects of ethnicity as equal: Italian-American is of roughly equivalent import as being Irish-American or African-American. But this false equivalence ignores the significant socially enforced structural inequality between some groups; people who are Italian-American or Irish-American have very different experiences in U.S. society compared to Mexican-Americans or African-Americans. Note these hierarchies changed over time; earlier in U.S.

history both Italian-Americans and Irish-Americans were viewed as inferior to others.

7. **Even the terminology we use defines a dominant group as a supposedly neutral standard.** For example, referring to people as non-white defines white as the standard, or referring to people as minority (even when they may be the statistical majority) defines the majority as the standard. This denies individuals in those groups the identity on their own terms without comparison to others. In what ways do we perceive our role in the socially constructed hierarchy?

See also: **Chapter 1:** Who Am I?

Chapter 4: What are My Values?

Chapter 5: How do I Define Myself?

Chapter 4.
What are My Values?

Have you ever wondered why you are always clashing with a particular person? Why they can never seem to understand your point of view or where you're coming from? More than likely, it's because you have different values. Values are standards by which an individual decides what is good, desirable, valuable, beautiful, etc. and that guide how they live their lives, make decisions, and move in the world.

1. **Values are developed as a result of the various influences within the groups** to which you have belonged over the course of your life. Your values can change over time.

2. **Groups such as family, friends and organizations, as well as influential factors such as mass media, determine your values.** Thinking about the various groups and circles to which you belong, what are the values that you think have helped to shape you?

3. **Examples of values include,** but are not limited to topics of: power, justice, wealth, equality, individualism, accountability, environmental protection, family importance, material success, charity, reliance on self, reliance on others and more. Is there one God, many gods, or no god? Is it ok to burn the American flag? Do you think eating meat is okay or morally wrong? Take a moment to write down some of your values. Glance at this list of 500 possible values, just to spark your thinking: https://www.threadsculture.com/core-values-examples

4. **Values, which are intangible aspects of culture, help to define our identity.** They help us decide what is right or wrong. Looking at some of the groups earlier mentioned in the first chapter, which groups do you think shaped and influenced your values?

5. **Are there any values within your circles that you feel do not align with your own values?** For example, many religions have values regarding gender roles or sexual orientations with which many members of those groups disagree. Consider situations in which you felt you "had" to make a certain decision based on your personal moral or ethical code. What values did those situations represent? Was this always the case? Add them to your list.

6. **Do you have strong political or religious beliefs that are vital to who you are?** If so, consider how this intersects with your values and among all the groups to which you belong.

7. **Here's where you will really drill down** – begin to group each of the values you've identified by theme/type – so honesty, integrity, and telling the truth might be things you've identified that go into one group, while laughter, fun, and play make up a second group. Chances are you will now have a list of 5-10 things that are vitally important to you, your happiness and your sense of purpose and fulfillment. While some people suggest rank-ordering these, that's a personal choice. If it's on the list, it matters, and that's the goal.

8. **Keep your values list handy and review it periodically.** The list can be updated as you need, consulted when you have a big decision to make, or shared with others to enable discussion and closeness.

See also: **Chapter 1:** Who Am I?

Chapter 3: Who are My People?

Chapter 5: How do I Define Myself?

Chapter 5.
How do I Define Myself?

As mentioned earlier, your identity is something that you get to define. It is what makes you distinct and unique from others. You develop an identity through reflection and integration of the perceptions of others -- because we care how we are perceived by others. Our identity can be somewhat different from how we choose to define ourselves.

1. **Aspects of your identity include,** but are not limited to, gender, ethnicity, religion, class, age, sexual orientation, profession, place of origin, dis/ability, and much more.

2. **Everyone has multiple identities.** These identities can be racial, ethnic, regional, organizational, national, language-centered and so much more. What are your various identities? Are some more meaningful or significant to you than others? If so, why do you think that's so?

3. **Although we often generalize for the sake of classification** (humans just love classifying things and people), there are no two individuals in the world with the exact same culture dynamic. But the important thing for you to know is that your identity influences you and guides both your expectations, actions, and responses to the norms and social rules in your organization.

4. **There are also different ways we can refer to aspects of ourselves, which can affect how we like to be referred to.** For example, someone who is Cuban-American could prefer Latinx over Latino or Hispanic, or they could prefer none of those and want to be referred to as Cuban. Many groups get lumped together to make it easier for people who are

not in those groups, but that negates part of the identify of people who are in those groups. Examples include Latinx/Hispanic, Asians, people of African descent, white people, and LGBTQ. Are you in any of these groups and prefer a specific description or nomenclature? Do you ever lump others into a general group instead of asking them how they like to be referred to?

5. **Here's an exercise you can try with a friend or a trusted co-worker** — preferably someone of a different cultural identity. Make a list of as many of your identities as you can. Draw a pie chart and assign to each portion of the chart a different identity. Each identity should receive space on the chart that is proportion to the importance of that particular identity to you. Discuss your findings with your friend or colleague. Was there anything surprising on your chart or theirs?

6. **Think about a time when someone may have mispronounced your name.** How did you feel? Perhaps you thought nothing about it the first time, but repeated mispronunciations may have disturbed you. Names are very important to our identity. And imagine if someone misgendered you or referred to you as a race or ethnicity or religion you were not. That adds up.

7. **How you self-identify influences how people interact with you.** It influences how people approach you or why they may choose to distance themselves from you. This is very important in the workplace.

8. **In years past, many people have chosen to self-identity as something other than how they were raised.** For example, light-skinned Black people often chose to pass as white in order to avoid discrimination and oppression during slavery and the Jim Crow era. Many times, these were desperate decisions made for reasons of safety, security, advancement, and to avoid discrimination. Can you name any instances that

you know of personally or have heard of where people have chosen to self-identify differently for personal or professional reasons?

See also: **Chapter 13:** Understanding Diversity of Race and Ethnicity

Chapter 14: Understanding Diversity of Gender

Chapter 15: Understanding Diversity of Sexual Orientation

Chapter 6.
I'm Not Biased! (Am I?)

The short answer is: 'Yes, you are biased.' *Everyone* is biased. To be biased means that you favor one person, group or thing over another. It means that you have a preference for something or someone. And while having preferences can be as harmless as choosing strawberry ice cream over butter pecan, with regard to diversity, they are definitely not. When we operate with biases—whether conscious or unconscious—in our world, we can discriminate against others and undermine our own values.

1. **Although there are different types of biases, most fall into two categories.** These are unconscious biases and conscious biases. Both of these biases can be present in the workplace and are detrimental to not just the organization but can also affect your own job performance when interacting with such individuals or when you exercise your own biases.

2. **Conscious bias is when individuals acknowledge and openly admit that they do not want to interact with certain individuals or groups of people based on their culture.** For example, some people prefer for their children to be in school with others who are of their same race/ethnicity. Other people prefer to associate only with people in their religious community and do not develop relationships with people outside their community. Have you witnessed anyone who displayed a conscious bias? How did you feel about it?

3. **Unconscious bias happens when the offender doesn't realize that they are operating with preferences for one individual or group of people while excluding another group or individual.** This goes beyond whether someone is a friend or not a friend and includes unconscious decisions about the

worth of people. We all have unconscious biases. For example, confirmation bias is the inclination to draw conclusions about a situation or person based on your personal desires, beliefs and prejudices rather than on the merit of the situation or person. Thinking back over your recent interactions with co-workers or classmates, have you preferred someone or a group of people over others? Why do you think you had a preference? If you included the other person or group, what do you think would have been different about the situation?

4. **Biases affect our attitude and how we act toward certain people.** Remember when we are in our work environment, managers, co-workers, and subordinates are always watching how we react to others. It's important to be conscious of how we include or exclude others, especially if we are doing so on the basis of their race, ethnicity, gender, religion, sexual orientation. Sometimes this bias could lead to discrimination against individuals.

5. **There are many ways to reduce bias, but – spoiler alert! – they all involve work.** The more we get to know ourselves, identify our biases, and come into contact with lots of different kinds of people and situations, the less our biases can take root. But we have to actively address our biases, check our facts, and consult with other people regarding our interpretations. In organizations, policies and practices (such as removing identifying information from a job candidate's materials that could bias people based on assumed ethnicity because of the candidate's name or setting diversity goals in the organization) can be helpful. See more in *Part 6: Leading Diversity, Equity, and Inclusion.*

See also: **Chapter 4:** What are My Values?

Chapter 7: My Stereotypes

Chapter 26: Pre-judgements and Prejudices

Chapter 7.
My Stereotypes

A *stereotype* is a widely held but fixed and oversimplified idea of a particular type of person, usually because of how they look. Some common stereotypes include "Children don't like healthy food," "All politicians are out for themselves," "Italians are the most romantic." What stereotypes do you have, and how can you address them? Read on ...

1. **Stereotyping is not only hurtful, it is also wrong.** Even if there is some truth behind the stereotype, it doesn't support the person's dignity to make assumptions about them based on preconceived perceptions. Stereotypes can encourage bullying and lead to disconnection and fear between people. Even if the stereotype is correct in some cases, constantly putting someone down based on your preconceived perceptions will not encourage them to succeed.

2. **Stereotypes influence our academic performance, the careers that we choose, our experiences at work, and how much we are paid for the work that we do.** What people believe about us affects how we move in the world. Stereotypes are associated with violence as well: People who stereotype LGBTQ individuals, women, or immigrants with specific negative characteristics are more likely to commit verbal or physical violence against those people.

3. **Stereotypes often don't make sense:** For example, some people in the U.S. believe that immigrants are both lazy people who don't work *and* people who are taking all the jobs from "real Americans." This is ridiculous!

4. **We can greatly reduce stereotyping others by first recognizing and making an assessment of the stereotypes**

we hold. This involves uncovering stereotypes you hold about others. In *Chapter 2: What is my culture?* we reviewed thoughts you have about what people *should* do. Look back at that list or start another list to identify how many of those are assumptions that may not be true.

5. **Meeting new people, especially people who are different from you, is also a good stereotype-buster, as long as you work at it.** Make sure that as you learn about people, you identify stereotypes you might have and identify whether they seem true for that person. In addition, ask the person what stereotypes they might have about any of your identities. For example, when I (JPW) travel internationally, people often tell me that I am not what they expect from an American. It's a great opportunity to discuss our stereotypes, how stereotypes emerged, and how they are/are not accurate.

6. **It's useful to approach these situations with some cultural humility.** Cultural humility involves learning to understand our own perspectives as we learn about theirs, reducing power imbalance, entering into mutual relationships including shared self-disclosure, and working for broader change.

7. **Knowing vs. believing.** It's ok to be aware of stereotypes – and to laugh at stereotypes about your own identities – but that's different from actually believing them. As you work to meet diverse people and intentionally learn and challenge yourself, you will become more comfortable disbelieving stereotypes that aren't helpful to true connection with other people.

See also: **Chapter 2:** What is My Culture?

Chapter 8: My Worldview

Chapter 10: Why Diversity Matters

Chapter 8.
My Worldview

As of this writing, there are 7.8 billion people on the earth. And believe it or not, we are all somehow in some small, wee, and tiny way, connected to one another. This may be hard to believe, particularly when we consider the distance between people who live in Rosario, Argentina and those living in Xinghua, China is over 12,425 miles. But worldviews overlap more often than we know.

1. **Essentially, worldviews are how groups of people explain life.** A worldview is how people interpret their reality with events and images of themselves which impacts how they relate to others.

2. **Your culture — your socially learned and transmitted behavior—shapes your worldview.** Specific examples of worldviews include religion, one's understanding of creation, what people think about death and the afterlife, ethics, perception of gender, and other philosophical issues concerning the existence of humanity.

3. **Traditionally, worldviews are rarely discussed directly – they're assumed.** People usually hold their worldviews in high regard and are often passionate about them. This is why many workplaces have discouraged people from discussing religion and politics as bosses often feel it may interfere with the relationships between employees.

4. **As our world becomes more multicultural, people are often more broad-minded and accepting of the worldviews of others even if they differ from their own understanding of life.** Thinking about your home, workplace, or school, did you or your peers openly discuss worldviews such as religion? How did it make you feel?

5. **Some worldviews may be challenging to address in work situations.** For example, some cultures take a very flexible view of time, where "let's meet at 8" could mean meeting anywhere between 8:30 and 10. For people who view time as much more rigid, this could be interpreted as the other person doesn't care or is unprofessional. In what other ways might worldviews be challenges in work situations? How do you think someone's worldview might interfere with their job performance? How can that be addressed in a workplace?

6. **When we study other cultures, we do so from the perspective of our own culture.** In other words, we can't help but view others through our own lens which is shaped by our own values and beliefs. It's like a fish who doesn't know it's in water! Because we arrive with beliefs and values which have already shaped our perspective, our view of the others and their culture is never fully accurate. And we automatically assume our views (of time, money, modesty, etc.) are the "norm." When you consider outsiders, or those who are not a part of your culture, it's important to interpret through our own lenses, and to understand some of our deep assumptions might not be assumed by everyone. Often when we explore these issues, we find we agree more with other people's ways of doing things rather than our own!

See also: **Chapter 2:** What is My Culture?

Chapter 10: Why Diversity Matters

Chapter 18: Understanding Diversity of Religion & Worldviews

Part 2.
Understanding Diversity

Chapter 9.
What is Diversity?

Diversity is a given context or setting with varying and unique aspects. When we speak about diversity in our society or in the workplace, we are referring to the variety of unique individuals being recognized for their differences. These differences can include race, ethnicity, gender, sexual orientation, age, religious beliefs, physical abilities, socio-economic status and more.

1. **Diversity is categorized in multiple ways.** A good way to think about diversity is to consider diversity in occupation, skills and abilities, personality traits, and values. People embody many different aspects—from the obvious (e.g., race) to the not-so-obvious (e.g., political views) – of diversity. Occupational diversity occurs when an individual changes their behavior based on their job and their position/role. Difference in skills and abilities is when people shift their behavior to utilize their strengths rather than their weaknesses. Personality traits are the individual's behaviorally consistent tendencies such as being energetic or being a perfectionist. Valuing diversity is respecting and embracing an individual's differences.

2. **Cultural diversity, also known as multiculturalism, can be defined as an acceptance and acknowledgement of individuals coming from different cultures, races, or ethnicities.** Embracing cultural diversity includes respecting individual differences, acknowledging and celebrating these differences. It allows diverse groups to feel empowered to be

seen and heard whether in their workplace, education setting, daily life, and within society as a whole.

3. **Diversity education is the concept where students embrace the differences in their classmates -- from social class to race -- as resources to broaden their education.** The diversity in a classroom setting can be an asset for individuals to see various perspectives within the education context, but it's also important to apply this broadened viewpoint into the real world.

4. **To promote diversity, respect each individual's differences.** Be open-minded to the various ways that people solve problems, perform a task, engage within a group setting, etc. Note this isn't "tolerating" differences, which means you are allowing the others to exist or enduring their existence. No one wants to be merely endured! True respect means you have regard and admiration for others.

5. **Difference is good.** Sometimes we tend to think different is bad and similar is good. Differences allow us to be more open-minded, push us to grow, and bring our different perspectives to real world problems.

6. **Diversity is all about connection.** As we each bring our individual differences to the table, we also want to connect with others. We connect with others when we embrace them as they are with non-judgmental curiosity.

7. **Bring more diversity into your life.** It might be joining a group from different cultures or listening to a podcast about different sexual orientations. There are so many possibilities in our society to welcome diversity into our daily lives.

8. **Workplace diversity is the concept of the various differences described above, interacting with one another for the common goal of the team or the mission of the company.** The similarities and differences of individuals

in a workplace can be an asset. It is only a hinderance when individuals fail to connect and communicate with respect.

See also: **Chapter 2:** What is My Culture?

Chapter 10: Why Diversity Matters

Chapter 11: Equality vs. Equity

Chapter 10.
Why Diversity Matters

Diversity matters because studies show that diverse teams are creative and high performing teams. Remember, diversity refers to the individual differences that are associated with someone's race (which is a social construct), ethnicity (which is usually self-identified), religious affiliation, national origin, age, sexual orientation, socioeconomic status, gender identity, language, and physical/mental abilities. Diversity matters because there is strength in the differences of individuals when they come together for a common goal.

1. **Diverse communities and workplaces have the advantage of a synergy of the varied ideas and experiences from different people who bring new and fresh ideas to the table**. Diverse people bring different perspectives. As a result, your team gains creativity and innovation. If you have a group of people representing four generations, with different countries of origin, representing various socio-economic sectors, you are bound to have a wide range of ideas and viewpoints which offer great value. The key is an environment that encourages a respectful and healthy dialogue of questions, thoughts and recommendations with the purpose of moving the company bottom line.

2. **We live in a global community.** Diverse teams enable you and your team to expand your footprint in the global market. Even if you're not currently doing business overseas, think about clients and customers in different regions of our country or even in your state where diversity at your company can have a positive impact on clients, customers and your community.

3. **Diversity allows for the interaction with others who are different.** Interaction with others who are different is the

main way to break down cultural barriers. These cultural barriers are hinderances to a productive work environment. Have you ever had to interact and complete a project with someone who was culturally different? If yes, how did you feel. If not, do you think you would be open to such an interaction or collaboration?

4. **Community satisfaction increases when a diverse group of people begins to work together toward a common goal.** Satisfaction increases because just by *being a diverse group*, you're letting an ever-increasing multicultural public know that you value and reflect who they are.

5. **A diverse workplace allows individuals to learn from others who are culturally different.** People tend to gravitate to people who are like them because it makes them feel comfortable. But constantly learning and having a growth mindset is crucial in today's fast-moving, global marketplace. What better way to expand your knowledge-base than by simply showing up to work and engaging with co-workers?

6. **Studies have proven that empathy is an important component in the workplace and in our communities.** Diverse groups allow interaction and exposure to others which builds empathy. Empathy allows us to embrace our differences which leads to a productive environment.

7. **While diversity greatly matters, inclusion is also key.** A diverse workforce that doesn't employ inclusion practices performs a great disservice and may very well counteract the advantages. See *Chapter 12: What is Inclusion?*

See also: **Chapter 9:** What is Diversity?

Chapter 39: Setting Workplace Diversity Goals

Chapter 44: Leveraging your Power to improve Diversity, Equity, and Inclusion

Chapter 11.
Equality vs. Equity

Historically, individuals battling discrimination have fought for the equality of all people. It has been determined, however, that equal treatment does not level the playing field when groups which have historically been discriminated against are beginning far behind the starting line that others have been warming up at for centuries. Equal opportunities and equal resources are often not enough when the disadvantaged group doesn't have the proper skills, education, and lack a clear understanding of the cultural norms and expectations of the dominant group in power.

1. **Equality** is a circumstance in which all people in a group or society have the same status, rights, freedoms and access to resources. **Equity** takes into consideration that diversity factors (e.g., race, gender) affect equality; equity provides disadvantaged individuals what they need so they can succeed, even if this means some people get more resources than others. For example, equality is when a teacher gives each child one apple; equity is when the teacher gives more food to those who are hungry and less food to those who brought their own lunch, so that all children are fed.

2. **When we embrace equity in the workplace, rather than equality, then we give people the resources they need to be successful.** Sometimes this provides resources individuals may not have ever experienced, such as mentorship. This is not equality where we treat everyone the same. The goal of equity is to give people a fair chance. One example of equity is offering extra accommodations for people with physical and mental health challenges. While the work environment will not be equal for those who are able-bodied and without a mental health illness, the environment will be equitable. Equity is

important because everyone deserves the opportunity to share their unique gifts, talents and perspective with the world.

3. **To promote equity, get to know people as individuals.** Understand that what we "bring to the table," might be vastly different. Know also that this can be a sensitive topic; we've probably all heard of the person who was born on third base but thought he hit a triple. Sometimes we are not aware of our privilege.

4. **Get to know your neighbors and colleagues and associates.** When you get to know them, you may find out that an "equal" playing field does not create parity when equal access is unavailable.

5. **Identify instances where perceived equality is being practiced and cultivate awareness.** One example might be scheduling a retreat on Friday evening or on a Saturday. Observant Jews or Seventh Day Adventists would not be able to attend a function scheduled at these times. Including diverse voices in decisions will ensure that equity is being practiced and not just equality. Including diversity in voices and practices will help people develop a broader understanding and respect for our differences.

6. **Partner and socialize with others who are culturally different so that you can gain an understanding of the challenges and obstacles they face.** This will give you a greater understanding of why equity is necessary rather than equality.

7. **Equity incorporates culture as a strength, not a complicator.** It can be challenging to adjust to so much difference in the world. For people who have typically been in privileged groups (e.g., white, male), it may seem like all of this diversity complicates everything. Being able to view diversity as a complication *is* a privilege because most people aren't able to choose how to consider diversity. Far from being a complicator, we suggest that equity can ensure that

our culture includes a glorious diversity of people, language, skin color, experiences, values, and approaches that make us stronger together.

8. **Equity can play an important role when making policies and procedures in the workplace.** By reviewing the differences of equality vs. equity described above, an individual could start to incorporate these tools into their workplace. One way to start is to look through the lenses of inequity and pro-equity and how you as an employee can impact your workplace environment by bringing awareness, policies, tools, etc. to the table with your colleagues.

See also: **Chapter 10:** Why Diversity Matters

Chapter 21: Privilege

Chapter 40: Increasing Representation in the Pipeline

Chapter 12.
What is Inclusion?

Inclusion is an effort and practice to ensure that people who have different backgrounds are culturally and socially accepted, welcomed, and treated equally. Inclusion goes beyond "tolerance" of diversity and ensuring an equitable workplace; it calls for actively embracing differences, empowering the inherent worth and dignity of all people, and ensuring everyone is welcome.

1. **Inclusive cultures make people feel respected and valued for who they are as individuals or groups.** People feel a level of supportive energy and commitment from others so that they can do their best at work. Inclusion often means a shift in mindset and culture in the community or workplace that has visible effects, such as representation on leadership committees, how space is physically organized, or the sharing of information.

2. **Inclusion is important because evidence shows that when people feel valued, they function at a higher capacity and feel part of the community or company.** This culture shift creates higher performing communities where motivation, morale, and impact are greatly increased.

3. **Inclusion in the workplace allows all employees equal access to opportunities and resources.** By having a supportive work environment, it gives all employees the ability to succeed and make a contribution that is valued within their company.

4. **In our society, inclusion is important as it gives individuals a sense of belonging.** When an individual feels accepted and embraced by others, it opens the door for empowerment and success.

5. **Be more mindful of inclusive language in your daily life.** Whether at work or with friends it's helpful to be aware of the language you're using and notice if it's inclusive or not. "Hey guys," is a phrase often used to refer to both men and women, which can feel excluding towards women and it can easily be changed to "Hey everyone."

6. **To be more inclusive, identify when you are making assumptions, and try to avoid assumptions.** When we make assumptions about someone's gender, sexual orientation, etc. we immediately make them feel excluded. Being aware of these assumptions can help us make corrections in the future and become more inclusive.

7. **To be inclusive is a continual process.** Be open and aware of areas in your life you might want to learn more about and connect with individuals or groups who can help your process. Read books and articles, listen to podcasts, and do your own work to understand others. Being inclusive is ongoing throughout every area of our lives.

8. **Evaluate your behavior.** Determine if you have inclusive behavior or not and in what areas do you notice it's not incorporated. Inclusive behavior includes all of the aspects listed above as well as many others and it's a good place to start the process.

See also: **Chapter 25:** Being an Ally and an Advocate

Chapter 26: Pre-judgements and Prejudices

Chapter 27: Intentional Communication

Part 3.
Understanding Others

Chapter 13.
Understanding Diversity of Race and Ethnicity

Few subjects bring up as much angst these days as race. From Black Lives Matter to White Guilt and everything in between, many of us have strong feelings about the topic of race.

1. **What are race and ethnicity?** Race and ethnicity are terms used to categorize people. In basic terms, race describes physical behaviors and cultural attributes. Ethnicity recognizes differences between people mostly on the basis of language and shared culture. In the U.S., the federal government recognizes five categories of race: *American Indian or Alaska Native, Asian, Black or African American, Native Hawaiian or Other Pacific Islander, White,* and *Some Other Race.* The U.S. government recognizes *"Hispanic or Latino"* as an ethnicity, not a race. In the U.S., therefore, individuals are a combination of the two: White and Hispanic/Latino, Black and non-Hispanic/Latino, and so on. In other countries where there is much more mixing of races and ethnicities, such as Brazil, most people are considered mixed. In the U.S., additional heritage is referred to on federal forms as "Ancestry," and can include Alsatian, British, Cambodian, Congolese, Dutch, Indian, South African, Swedish, and so on.

2. **As happens with gender, many categories of race and ethnicity are often lumped into one imperfect category.** For example, the term "Hispanic" refers to people from Spain and Latin American Spanish-speaking countries. Similar terms include "Latino/a," "Latinx" (to address the gender inherent in Spanish language and provide a gender-neutral version), and "Chicano/a" to refer to individuals from Mexico. Of course,

people of Spanish origin may have nationalities or ancestry from Spain, Argentina, or Costa Rica, and may also be mixed heritage with colonists from various European countries and indigenous peoples. Lumping all people from Spain and Latin America into "Hispanic" or "Latino/a" erases important differences including nationality, heritage, language, and culture.

3. **The worldwide scourge of slavery brought African individuals to the U.S. and systematically denied their freedom, education, and voting rights,** first through enslavement then through denial of civil rights and now through often more subtle discrimination and racism. If we make assumptions that race is just value neutral categories, it negates the painful fact that not everyone came to the U.S. voluntarily.

4. **Racism and Discrimination.** Racism is prejudiced thoughts or discriminatory actions based on race, usually by people of white/European descent toward people of color. Discrimination is the behavioral correlate of racism: the denial of justice and fair treatment by individuals or institutions in many areas including employment, education, housing, banking, and civil rights. Racist thoughts are likely to lead to discriminatory actions. These thoughts don't necessarily mean we're bad people, but it's important to continue to learn and grow and let those negative assessments of others go so that we can respect others as whole people. Racism is pervasive and can contribute to us supporting structures that enact overtly racist policies and practices. When we can understand and change our unconscious racism, bias, and discrimination in ourselves, we can begin to shift the societal structures that perpetuate racism. Racism doesn't just oppress non-whites, it oppresses *all* of us because it robs us of an equal, diverse, and loving society.

5. **Affirmative Action is the policy and practice of favoring individuals in groups who have previously been**

discriminated against. Essentially, it means taking intentional steps now to address the wrongs of the past. In the U.S. in 1966, President Lyndon Johnson ordered contractors to take "affirmative action" to ensure that applicants and employees are treated equally during employment, without regard to their race, color, religion, sex, or national origin. In 1969, President Richard Nixon promised affirmative action in government employment. Some people feel affirmative action is merely a quota system for promoting under-qualified minorities; they feel it's not fair that others get a boost at their expense because they personally did not cause the inequality. Others identify that it is the responsibility of a government to pursue equity, not just equality, when there has been systematic discrimination. Affirmative action is an enormous topic, and court cases are changing perceptions of affirmative action. You may want to learn more about your state and company's affirmative action guidelines, and read about ongoing court cases related to affirmative action.

6. **Some people assert there are significant differences between races with regard to educational achievement, intelligence, and other factors.** Although this was a topic of big concern in the 1800s and 1900s – especially to white men eager to "prove" their superiority – there is little evidence that any racial group, however defined, is superior to any others in these ways. There is much more within-group difference (e.g., among White people) than between-group difference (e.g., between White people and Black people). Culture, nationality, socio-economic status, and opportunity explain most differences more than race itself.

7. **Black Lives Matter vs. All Lives Matter: What's going on?** Black Lives Matter is a decentralized political and social movement that protests police brutality and racial violence against Black people. The movement emerged in the late 2010s in response to increasing incidents of police violence against Black people. Some people have responded to "Black Lives

Matter," with "All Lives Matter," which serves to change the focus from the importance of Black lives to pretending that all lives are valued equally, which they are not. These people interpret the phrase to mean "Black Lives Matter (more)," which they interpret as offensive, whereas the phrase actually intends to assert "Black Lives Matter (as well)."

8. **White guilt** is individual or collective guilt felt by some white people because of harm their ancestors caused against people of color, including slavery, genocide, and colonialism). Some argue that white guilt is associated with a stronger desire to support people of color and affirmative action initiatives. White guilt can be problematic in that it can lead white people to focus on getting acceptance and forgiveness from people of color rather than changing their own actions or beliefs.

9. **Making change.** Some people feel that diversity, equity, and inclusion is not their problem, so they have no role in improving it. This is completely false. Diversity, equity, and inclusion are goals for everyone, and all people regardless of how they identify can step up in many ways and use their power and privilege to make significant improvements. Ways everyone can contribute are: join or start a diversity committee, talk with your children about race, get to know more people of color (and don't ask them to educate you), challenge your own stereotypes, and speak up when you see injustice. The more you know about yourself and about others, the more you can use your feelings and experiences to help make the world a better place.

See also: **Chapter 7:** Stereotypes

            Chapter 11: Equality vs. Equity

            Chapter 25: Being an Ally and an Advocate

Chapter 14.
Understanding Diversity of Gender

For most people in the world, gender is the first salient characteristic people want to know. Everyone asks pregnant women: "Is it a boy or a girl?" Once gender is known, most of us breathe a sigh of relief that we know that she will be sweet and cuddly and adorable or that he will be tough and strong. Really? You would think that we as a global community would be past this by now. But in many communities, your gender determines how you should act, the aspirations you should have, and even how much you're allowed to operate independently. And that's just getting started. Take a walk with us down a brief foray into gender…

1. **What are the genders?** People can be male or female, which are usually designated by our sex characteristics (having a penis or a vagina); this is called gender assigned at birth. There are some people for whom gender at birth is indeterminate; these individuals are generally referred to as intersex and may be raised in a single gender. For those who identify as the gender you were assigned at birth, you are considered cisgender. People can also be non-binary (neither male nor female) and agender (someone who doesn't identify with the idea or experience of having a gender).

2. **People can also change from male to female (transgender MTF) or female to male (transgender FTM).** Note that transgender individuals may or may not have had gender confirmation surgery (also called sex reassignment surgery). Some transgender individuals identify only as their gender (male or female) and others identify as transgender. Also note it's none of your business -- ever -- whether anyone has had surgery on their genitals or takes hormones. Unless you're a

51

physician about to conduct gender confirmation surgery, it is never an appropriate question to ask! You can ask about what pronouns the person uses (he/him, she/her, or they/them), and use those.

3. **Gender identity is the way someone experiences gender internally as part of their core sense of self.** Gender identity can't be assumed based on appearance, anatomy, social norms, or stereotypes. Gender identity isn't determined by assigned gender or sex, and can develop or change over time.

4. **People request to be referred to using the pronouns that match their conception of their gender.** I may prefer to be referred to as "she/her" if I identify as female, "he/him" if I identify as male, or "they/them" if I am nonbinary. Use "they/them" also if you don't know the person's gender. In the olden days, "he/him" was used to refer to the generic person of either gender, such as "mankind" referring to all people. These days, that's not appropriate, as "mankind" refers to men and "humanity" refers to people of all genders. It was a big deal when the New York City Metropolitan Transit Authority (its bus and subway system) changed its announcements from starting "Ladies and gentlemen..." to starting with, "Everyone..." Kudos! Even though you may not fully understand what it means for someone to identify as non-binary, it is important that you respect how others choose to self-identify.

5. **Show your support for non-binary co-workers by using your own pronouns in your email signature behind your name or when you are speaking on a panel or about to give a public speech.** For example, as a cisgender individual (one who identifies with the sex assigned at birth), I (LDJ) show my support for those who are non-binary by listing my name as "Dr. Lisa D. Jenkins (she/her/hers)." You can do the same. It's a small step that can be enormously reassuring to people who are nonbinary. Always refer to the Golden Rule. If you

were socialized in an environment that did not or does not recognize people who are non-binary, it's important that you simply do unto others as you would have them to do unto you. In other words, as you would like to be referred to in a certain way, remember that others desire the same and deserve the same respect.

6. **Although there are many aspects of gender that differentiate the experience of individuals who are male, female, and non-binary, two of the most pervasive and dangerous aspects are violence against women and the health risks of childbirth.** People may argue about whether women or men are better at math or leadership, or which sex is more aggressive, more empathic, more sexually active, more emotional, or myriad issues. Ultimately, however, most gender "differences" often display more variation within gender (e.g., among men) than across genders (e.g., between women and men). Not so for violence against women and childbirth, which are both significant global public health issues that affect many people around the world, including cisgender women, transgender individuals, and others assumed female based on their appearance.

7. **Both men and women face significant gender role expectations, which are societal expectations on how we are supposed to act based on our (perceived) gender.** For example, men are supposed to demonstrate strength and not emotion, whereas women are supposed to be nurturing and kind. These move into challenges in development, because it's difficult to learn who we truly are with all of these expectations on how we *should* behave, as well as challenges in the workplace. For example, how people describe "leaders" is also how people describe "men" and very different from how people describe "women." Women, more than men, are punished when we stray from expected gender roles. Note these roles may be more or less rigid depending on other aspects of your identity, such as nationality or religion.

8. **Patriarchy is a system of society or government in which men hold power, political leadership, moral authority, social privilege and control of property, and women are largely excluded from this power.** This creates problems for *all* genders because of gender role expectations that harm male- and female-identifying people, low tolerance for resisting gender expectations, lack of fair opportunities for individuals, unequal justice, and unequal application of violence toward women and nonbinary people. Patriarchy is embedded in our social structure so that individuals who benefit from patriarchy assume it's because they are better or more worthy; any attempt to make society more equal feels to them like they are being discriminated against.

9. **Feminism is the advocacy of women's rights based on the fundamental equality of the genders.** It is not "anti-men"; it is merely against the system that stacks the deck so women are continually disadvantaged.

10. **Rebecca Solnit defined "mansplaining" as when men explain things to women in a condescending or patronizing way.** Although mansplaining is hardly the most egregious of gender inequalities, it is pervasive in the Western world and incredibly annoying to women who already know what they're doing and do not want to experience men's overconfidence, arrogance, and condescension.

11. **To learn more about gender, identify the ways in which you relate to your gender.** Check out gender stereotypes (you can find lists on the internet), and identify whether you are like "most men" or "most women"? Or do you feel like you don't fit into either "male" or "female" categories? Once you've identified the stereotypes and how you agree or don't agree, consider what you experience when you behave differently than your stereotype would suggest (for example, if you are a woman firefighter or a male nurse, or a woman who is aggressive or a man who is shy). What is that like?

Can you imagine what it might be like to feel that way all the time?

See also: **Chapter 5:** How do I Define Myself?

Chapter 15: Understanding Diversity of Sexual Orientation

Chapter 21: Privilege

Chapter 15.
Understanding Diversity
of Sexual Orientation

LGBTQ -- there are lots of letters! For individuals who are sexual minorities (i.e., not heterosexual and cisgender), it's often a challenging experience to identify one's sexual orientation. Getting more specific about exactly how one identifies can be an important part of that journey.

1. **Homophobia, transphobia and transmisogyny are detrimental not only to the morale and productivity of the individual but can lead to depression, anxiety and even suicide.** They are all part of a patriarchal system that privileges men and maleness and punishes deviation from gender norms. This can have a profound negative effect on individuals who are LGBTQ.

2. **Let's break down the the full LGBTQIAP+ acronym (often abbreviated to LGBTQ):**

    a. **Lesbian:** A woman physically, romantically, and/or emotionally attracted to other women

    b. **Gay:** Gay people are those who are physically, romantically, and/or emotionally attracted to those of the same gender. It's used for both women and men. Some women prefer the word lesbian and some refer to themselves as gay. In the Black community, this is sometimes referred to as "same gender loving" or SGL.

    c. **Bisexual:** People who are physically, romantically, and/or emotionally attracted to both men and women are called bisexual. It's often abbreviated to 'bi'.

d. **Transgender:** Someone who identifies as a different gender than that of the body they were born in. Some use surgery and hormones to transition to the gender they're comfortable with and others do not. Note transgender is in the sexual orientation acronym, but it is actually a gender identity.

e. **Queer/Questioning:** Queer is an umbrella term used by individuals who are not heterosexual and who may view other terms as too limiting. The term "Queer" was previously an insult that has been reclaimed by the community, so use it cautiously when referring to others. Questioning refers to individuals who are in the process of understanding their sexual orientation or gender identity.

f. **Intersex:** An intersex person is someone who does not have distinct biological sex. It could be because of their reproductive organs, their chromosome patterns, or other reasons.

g. **Asexual:** A person who is asexual is someone who doesn't feel sexual desire. It varies from person to person as each person's sexuality is unique, but one should note that people who are asexual can have romantic or emotional attraction, can have a sex drive or sexual desire, and aren't necessarily celibate. They just have minimal to no sexual desire.

h. **Pansexual:** A person who is pansexual is someone who is physically, emotionally, and/or romantically attracted to all people, no matter their sex or gender identity. This is different from bisexual as bisexuals are attracted to men and women, while pansexuals can be attracted to people who are intersex or nonbinary or anywhere on the gender spectrum.

i. **Plus:** The "plus" can include anyone who doesn't identify as any of the other letters; it can also just mean an intentional inclusivity.

3. **Note that sexual orientation is different from gender identity.** People can identify as any gender and have any sexual orientation in any combinations. For example, a person who is transgender MTF could be attracted to men, women, or others. It's generally not appropriate to assume or ask about sexual orientation unless you are specifically interested in dating or having sex with them.

4. **For many individuals older than 40 years old in the U.S., people who grew up in very conservative/religious families, and people in many parts of the world today,** coming out can be a difficult process. Not only do we have societal expectations of our gender, when we get married (and to whom), who is appropriate to fall in love with, and how we should behave, we also have religion, nationality, and other parts of our identity that may also have their own perspectives on sexual orientation. In some parts of the world, homosexual sex is still against the law and can be punishable by death. In other cultures – including some in the U.S. – individuals who come out are shunned from their families, houses of worship, or communities.

5. **Our beliefs about sexual orientation relate strongly to our beliefs about gender.** Some groups state that it's wrong to be LGBTQ; others state it's okay to *be* LGBTQ as long as you don't *act* on those urges (e.g., to engage in a loving relationship with someone to whom you're attracted). What are your beliefs about sexual orientation? Where do those beliefs come from? Have you heard people make positive or negative comments about individuals who were presumed gay? If you think it's not okay to be gay, what do you think people who are gay should do? If you believe being LGBTQ is a choice, do you think you could change your sexual orientation? Why or why not?

6. **To learn more, seek out members of the LGBTQ community who are in your community or workplace and invite them to lunch.** You'd be surprised at how much you have in common! Talk about normal things (don't start

by asking them about sex). If you are unable to identify individuals who are part of the LGBTQ community at your workplace, you can go to organizations such as PFLAG (Parents and Friends of Lesbians and Gays), a local LGBTQ center, or Pride Month activities in June.

7. **Consider becoming an ally and advocate for LGBTQ people.** First learn about the community and the issues (check out the materials in the For Further Reading section), then ask people in the LGBTQ community how you can best support them. Something as small as speaking up when someone says, "That's so gay!" in a negative way or expresses negative comments about an LGBTQ person can make a big difference.

See also: **Chapter 5:** How do I Define Myself?

Chapter 15: Understanding Diversity of Gender

Chapter 21: Privilege

Chapter 16.
Understanding Diversity of Nationality/Immigration Status

One of the basic identities of an individual is their nationality and immigration status. Legal and approved immigration status in most countries can confer a right to work, obligations to pay taxes, and protection from random deportation; undocumented individuals or those in countries without legal immigration status can be subject to harassment, abuse, and deportation.

1. **In the United States, immigration status has four types: citizen, resident, non-immigrant, and undocumented.** Citizens are people who have been born in the U.S. or become naturalized. They cannot be deported unless they committed specific and significant fraud. Permanent residents have a green card to legally work and reside in the U.S. permanently. Conditional residents are people married less than 2 years before they are authorized a green card. Non-immigrants refer to foreign nationals who temporarily reside in the U.S. for a particular purpose, such as work, and who are not pursuing citizenship. Undocumented refers to people who are in the U.S. illegally or without permission (e.g., they overstayed their visa). There is a possibility for undocumented people to be deported at any given time. Note the terms "illegal immigrant" and "illegal alien" are considered dehumanizing, because they refer to the *person* as illegal, rather than the behavior. The term "undocumented" is more appropriate and respectful.

2. **Nationality** is defined as the country where you are a legal citizen or where you were born. An example of this would be if you were born in Russia and became a U.S. citizen you could consider your nationality as Russian, American, and/or

Russian-American. Nationality is where you feel a sense of belonging either in the country you were born and/or where you are a citizen.

3. **Dual Citizenship/Dual Nationality** is acceptable under U.S. law and allows people to be citizens of the U.S. and another country at the same time. Some countries do not allow dual citizenship.

4. **Nationality vs. citizenship:** Nationality is given by birth, adoption, or marriage. In the U.S., all individuals born in the U.S. are automatically U.S. citizens, and individuals in U.S. territories (e.g., American Samoa) are U.S. nationals. Citizenship gives an individual rights and responsibilities dependent on the legal relationship between the state and a person. An individual can be both a U.S. citizen and national; some individuals who are natives of U.S. territories may be a U.S. national but not a U.S. citizen. Nationals who aren't U.S. citizens can apply for a U.S. passport, have the right to protection by consular offices when they are traveling abroad, and are allowed to travel and live in the U.S. Nationals, however, don't qualify for many other benefits of U.S. citizenship, such as the right to vote in U.S. elections or apply for jobs that require U.S. citizenship.

5. **The U.S. Constitution grants rights to people in the U.S., which means undocumented immigrants have certain rights when they are in the U.S.** Some of these rights include freedom of religion and speech and the right to due process and equal protection under law. It gets complicated when these rights are put into practice and how they are worked out within our legal system. These rights can also vary between city, state, and federal law. For example, New York's state constitution ensures undocumented individuals have the right to shelter, but federal laws prohibit undocumented individuals' access to Medicaid or supplemental nutrition assistance.

6. **Legal rights granted are determined by an individual's immigration status.** As mentioned above, all people in the U.S. have rights no matter their status under the Constitution. It's important to know what your basic rights are as well as your rights depending on your immigration status.

7. **Immigration laws in the U.S. are complex.** It is important to do your research to properly understand the laws and rights you or others have depending on your immigration status. It can be an eye-opening experience to gain more knowledge about the process even if you are a U.S. citizen from birth.

8. **The U.S. was built on immigration, and immigration creates more diversity.** Immigrants bring innovative ideas and a new perspective whether it's in the workplace or in the community. Immigration helps make the world more connected and bring expansion into our culture. Everyone in the U.S. now except for Native Americans, was once a voluntary or involuntary immigrant.

9. **Knowledge is power.** The more you understand the U.S. system relating to immigration and learn more about what immigrants face on a daily basis, and the ways they contribute to our society, the more open-minded you will be. It can be empowering to know about the diverse group of people that make up the country you live in.

See also: **Chapter 1:** Who Am I?

Chapter 10: Why Diversity Matters

Chapter 25: Being an Ally and an Advocate

Chapter 17.
Understanding Diversity of Disability

The definition of a disability is any impairment of the mind or body making an individual with this condition to have activity limitations and/or participation restrictions. Major types of disabilities are hearing impairment, visual impairment, cognitive impairment, and/or motor (physical) impairment.

1. **People can experience a disability permanently or temporarily during some stage in their lifetime.** A person may be born with a physical disability that is permanent or a person might have a temporary physical disability due to an accident.

2. **Disability crosses all lines of diversity including gender, race, education, socioeconomic, and organization.** It's important to recognize that all people no matter their background or status can have a permanent or acquire a temporary disability. People with disabilities may experience multiple layers of discrimination depending on their gender, race, etc. See *Chapter 22: Intersectionality.*

3. **The Americans with Disabilities Act (ADA)** was created in 1990 to protect people with disabilities from unlawful discrimination in the workplace, transportation, public accommodation, communications, and government activities. It requires government organizations and public businesses (such as schools and stores) to provide reasonable accommodations for people with disabilities.

4. **Invisible disabilities** are disabilities that are not physically seen or immediately recognizable. These types of disabilities can include chronic pain, sleep disorders, mental illnesses, learning disabilities, etc. and they are not obvious to others.

People with invisible disabilities can be accused of imagining their disability and not receive the assistance they may need.

5. **People with disabilities can experience discrimination on a daily basis.** When a building or public space only has stairs, it makes it inaccessible to people with physical disabilities. Even with the ADA there are still many public spaces and buildings that do not comply and continue to discriminate against people with disabilities. See *Chapter 23: A guide to -isms.*

6. **Each category of disability comes with various stereotypes and severities of discrimination.** People with physical disabilities can be discriminated against as lazy or they can be stereotyped as extremely brave. People with mental illnesses can be discriminated by fears from others or looked down upon by society. There's a spectrum of discrimination depending on the type of disability a person has.

7. **It's important to dive deeper into individual's experiences with their disability.** Each person with a disability has a unique perspective and history of how they became disabled and their experience in daily life. It can help others let go of perceptions attached to disabilities and become more connected with the individual instead of the label.

8. **There's so much diversity in the disability community to recognize and acknowledge.** Becoming more familiar with what people with disabilities go through and the types of disabilities can help breakdown the stigmas and barriers in our society.

See also: **Chapter 7:** Stereotypes

Chapter 22: Intersectionality

Chapter 23: A guide to -isms

Chapter 18.
Understanding Diversity of Religion & Worldviews

Until recently, people did not talk about religion outside of their immediate circle of family or friends. Although now it is more acceptable to discuss religion, it can still be a touchy subject for some people. We often think of religious discrimination and oppression occurring in other countries, although that perspective is usually from a Western and Christian point of view. Religious discrimination has always been present in the U.S., and in recent decades, it has surged. While racial and ethnic discrimination are more obvious, we must be clear that the freedom of religion (the acceptance of different theological systems of belief) and the freedom of worship (the freedom of the individual action aligned with the belief) are important fundamental principles of our society, including the freedom to not have religious beliefs or actions. In the sociological context, we refer to religions and belief systems as worldviews.

1. **Consider the historical legacies of Christian hegemony imposed by early Europeans along with pervasive Christian norms.** Understand the seemingly "harmless" proselytization of missionaries who imposed their beliefs on Native Americans and other indigenous cultures, often while enslaving, abusing, raping, and murdering them. The assumption of Christian hegemony persists in incidents like posting the Ten Commandments outside of justice buildings and posting Nativity scenes on government property. If you're not sure how this is problematic, imagine if you were to talk into a courtroom to find the walls decorated with tenets of Islamic law, images of Buddhist gods decorating the building, or being asked to swear to tell the truth with one hand on the Book of Mormon. Would you feel that you would be treated fairly?

2. **Religions encompass much more than a belief in a God or multiple gods.** Most religions also describe a code of conduct (sometimes different for men and women), how one should spend money, how one works with neighbors, rules about with whom and how one can have sex, what is appropriate attire, what one can and can't eat, when and how one should worship, how to treat children and elders, important events and rituals, and more. For some people, they attend a house of worship occasionally and celebrate some holidays, whereas for others, all aspects of their lives are guided by their religion.

3. **Also consider the stereotypes and discrimination against people without religion, as many people disapprove of and condemn atheism and agnosticism.** This disapproval is especially true in geographical areas that are more homogenous across our country. Northeast and west coast populations are typically more open to individuals who worship differently or not at all.

4. **The U.S. has been erroneously described as a Judeo-Christian country.** "Judeo-Christian" is a term used to group Christianity and Judaism together. The founders of the U.S. were adamant about freedom to worship and freedom from any governmental interference with worship. Still, from its early days, U.S. settlers were not always tolerant of each other's religions, and Americans have displayed significant anti-Catholicism, anti-Semitism (against Jewish people), and anti-Muslim sentiments, including discrimination and violence.

5. **A good way to start learning about other religions is to publicly recognize religious holidays that are not associated with your worldview.** Do your research, discuss them with others, and use the opportunities to understand more fully the religious beliefs and stories that are central to the holidays.

6. **Learn about different attire people wear due to their beliefs – and their explanations for why they wear what they do.** For example, many people confuse men who are Sikh with

men who are Muslim because of their headwear, which can look similar to individuals who don't know the difference. Also, Muslim women wear a hijab (a veil which covers the head and chest and sometimes the face) for many different reasons.

7. **Discuss with friends or colleagues your interpretations of the U.S. Constitution's First Amendment,** which prohibits laws limiting freedom with respect to religion, expression, peaceful assembly or the right of citizens to petition the government. You could start with easy questions and progress to discussing whether it's okay to have prayer in school, the ten commandments posted in or outside a federal building, use sacred Native American lands for development, provide protections for less-common religions such as Latter Day Saints (Mormons), and the criteria to establish religions in the U.S. It is best if there are individuals present who represent different worldviews and religions, and of course, be respectful.

8. **Respect what others say about their religious identification and their experiences.** Even if you're not very religious, others are and take their beliefs and practices very seriously. Their *experience of religion and religiosity* might be very different from yours. Be aware of your own biases about various religions and worldviews, and stay curious as you learn about others.

See also: **Chapter 2:** What is My Culture?

Chapter 8: My Worldview

Chapter 26: Pre-judgements and Prejudices

Chapter 19.
Understanding Diversity of
Poverty and Wealth Inequality

Income inequality describes how uneven income is distributed throughout a population. Income inequality is often overshadowed by injustice; however, income inequality is often a *result* of racial, gender, and other injustices. Although no one will ever have the exact same income, income inequality refers to the uneven distribution based on systematic inequality related to racial, gender, geographic, disability or other factors.

1. **The U.S. has a long history of facilitating income and wealth inequality.** Median wealth of white families is 12 times higher than the median wealth of African American families. After slavery ended, for example, leaders created many ways to keep African Americans from earning comparable wages and accumulating wealth, including paying people of color less for the same job, redlining (refusing loans for homes in certain neighborhoods due to perception of risk that is also associated with the racial distribution of the neighborhood) and other forms of lending discrimination, and discrimination in educational opportunities that directly affect wealth. Until 1963, it was legal in the U.S. to pay women less than men for doing the same work. Non-discrimination laws are addressing these issues, but this is a multi-generational problem that is challenging to overcome.

2. **Recognize that peers and co-workers may be experiencing poverty or wealth inequality.** Just because you work with them, do not assume that their personal lives, financial

stability, familial experiences with money, and choices about spending and saving are comparable to yours.

3. **Realize that someone else's finances can vary greatly** depending on their race, gender, size of family, geographic location, gender, previously accumulated debt and loans, and much more. They may also be an outlier: do not assume someone is low income because of where they live or their race.

4. **Beware of conversations that might alienate others.** For example, while most people can't afford to go sailing on weekends, for some, taking a day trip might also be unaffordable because the cost of gas and lunch isn't in their budget. What might seem like a normal activity to one person may be out of reach for others.

5. **Try not to overcompensate if you are aware of a person's income inequality.** You may feel the need to "help" the individual with frequent offerings to pay for meals, etc. For many, this may be insulting. Unless you are extremely close to the individual and there is a clear understanding of intent, it is best to not extend yourself in this manner. Instead, seek opportunities to spend time together that do not involve money.

6. **Take steps to improve income inequality whenever possible.** For example, women still earn less than men in part because of disparities in hours worked, job experiences, parental responsibilities, and chosen occupation. Many workplaces have initiatives to address these issues. Learn about them and see what you can do to improve income inequality.

7. **Educate yourself about income inequality and wealth accumulation.** Learn about uneven wages between men and women; among ethnicities and races as well as neighborhoods. Ask yourself why these inequalities exist. Learn to connect the dots. This will help you develop empathy, which will lead to

more favorable relationships with those experiencing income inequality or poverty.

See also: **Chapter 13:** Understanding Diversity of Race and Ethnicity

Chapter 14: Understanding Diversity of Gender

Chapter 38: Building the Multicultural Workplace

Chapter 20.
Understanding Diversity of Age

For the first time in history, we have five different generations actively working. These include the Silent Generation (also known as the Traditionalists), born 1925 to 1945; the Baby Boomers, born 1946 to 1964; Generation X, born 1965 to 1980, Millennials, born 1981 to 2000; and Generation Z, born 2001 to 2020. Intergenerational communication, which is the interaction between two or more distinct generations, can be tricky because the culture of each generation dictates certain expectations and roles for individuals.

1. **In the U.S. laws against age discrimination are relatively recent (since 1967) and limited to individuals 40 and older.** There are no laws protecting people from being discriminated against because they're young. Further, even though age should generally not be discussed at work, many young people experience substantial negative comments about their (apparent) age, including, "I'm old enough to be your mother/father," assuming someone does not know something because of their age, assuming that if a young person doesn't know something it is due to ignorance or lack of will rather than never having been exposed to it, and multiple nonverbal gestures such as rolling eyes or scoffing at the term, "Millennial." Young people are further treated differently by "last in, first out" policies that lay off workers with shorter tenure first (usually younger people), and perceptions that young people without families are easier to lay off.

2. **People of different ages add innovation, stability, and perspective to groups and families.** It's important to have young people to add new ideas, and it's also important to have people who have more experience to provide stability, context, and perspective over time. If people work respectfully together,

75

they can pool their skills and emerge stronger.

3. **A good step toward understanding diversity of age is to identify and delete negative stereotypes of people based on their age.** Recognize that older people may view young people with reminiscence or disappointment about their own youth; younger people may experience anxiety about the inevitability of aging and the physical and cognitive changes it entails. Choose to look for exceptions to stereotypes, and don't make negative comments about other generations.

4. **Recognize different experiences lead to different perspectives.** Someone who grew up during the Vietnam War will likely have a different perspective on public protests than someone who is experiencing them for the first time now. Ask people of different ages about their experiences when they were in their teens, 20s, and 30s, and ask how those experiences affected them. Hearing that when my (JPW) mother was 20, women weren't legally allowed to open bank accounts without their husband's approval, or that when my grandmother was 20, women weren't expected to finish high school definitely provides a different perspective on what I experienced when I was 20 or what 20 year-olds today experience!

5. **Find opportunities to communicate frequently.** Consider ways in which there can be perceived intergenerational conflict, such as progressive vs. traditional views, believing one earned benefits vs. others who feel entitled, and focusing on "me" vs. "we." Instead of making assumptions, ask questions about what people are thinking and feeling, and have the difficult conversations.

6. **Identify ways to learn from other generations.** Who doesn't love a good "When I was your age…" story? Millennials can learn from older generations about their experiences growing up in a very different world than what we have now, and can benefit from their perspectives on how work, companies, and processes changed over the years. People older than us

often have a better understanding of workplace and cultural politics as well. Similarly, Millennials have perspectives and experiences about the world that can be valuable to people older and younger than them (and not just about technology).

7. **Offer to teach people from other generations.** Millennials and Generation Z have much to offer older generations, and again, not just about technology. Younger generations have different perspectives of current events, and often more open views of interpersonal relationships. There are many opportunities Millennials and Generation Z have to share knowledge with others to help them feel more informed and more comfortable in the world.

See also: **Chapter 7:** Stereotypes

Chapter 23: A guide to -isms

Chapter 40: Increasing Representation in the Pipeline

Chapter 21.
Privilege

Privilege is a special right, advantage, or immunity granted or available only to a particular person or group. For example, the privilege to travel freely throughout the world is limited to individuals of certain nationalities, genders, and wealth. Privilege is a function of multiple variables of varying importance, such as race, age, gender, etc. Race and gender often have the most impact because they are usually immediately visible; some aspects of privilege (such as education, wealth and attractiveness) may change over time.

1. **The concept of white privilege comes from a 1988 essay of the same name by Peggy McIntosh** The essay clarifies tangible benefits to being white, such as being able to easily find shampoo for your kind of hair and being able to turn on the television and see people of your race widely represented. There has been some backlash against the concept of white privilege, especially from white people of low socio-economic status who resent being called "privileged" (and are not used to being profiled by their race – another form of privilege). Generally white privilege means having greater access to power and resources than people of color [in the same situation] do." There are other forms of privilege, of course, including male privilege and straight privilege.

2. **A clear, compelling, and disturbing example of privilege involves a May 25, 2020 Central Park incident in which a white woman called police on an African American man because he asked her to leash her dog.** She told the police that he was attacking her, when in fact he was simply standing near her. Fordham Professor of Theological and Social

Ethics Bryan N. Massingale observed that the white woman demonstrated many examples of white privilege, including:

a. She assumed her lies would be more credible than his truth.

b. She assumed that she would have the presumption of innocence and that he would have the presumption of guilt.

c. She assumed that the police would back her up.

d. She assumed that her race would be an advantage, because she is white, and that his race would be a burden.

e. She assumed that she had the upper hand in the situation.

f. She assumed that she could exploit deeply ingrained fears of African-American men.

g. She assumed that if he protested his innocence against her, he would be seen as "playing the race card." She assumed that no one would accuse her of "playing the race card," because no one accuses white people of playing the race card when using race to their advantage.

h. She assumed that he knew that any confrontation with the police would not go well for him.

i. She assumed that the frame of "black rapist" versus "white damsel in distress" would be clearly understood by the police, the press, and the public.

j. She assumed that a African-American man had no right to tell her what to do – and that the police officers would agree.

k. She assumed that even if the police made no arrest, that a lot of white people would take her side and believe her anyway.

3. **It may seem like there are more incidents like this in the news, but the difference is only in that they can now be recorded and shared to social media.** Incidents like the Central Park situation have happened throughout the U.S., and many people of color, like Emmett Till in 1955, have not always had the fortune of recording devices or the ability to emerge with their lives.

4. **There is an exercise called the Privilege Walk that has individuals line up in a row and then step forward or backwards in response to statements about privilege,** such as "If you grew up speaking English at home, take one step forward," and "If you took out loans for your education, take one step backwards." The exercise can be powerful. Criticisms of the exercise are that it relies on people of less privilege to provide the learning opportunity for people of more privilege, and that it may shame people with more privilege. Nevertheless, it may be useful as a discussion tool rather than an exercise.

5. **Most people are reluctant to acknowledge their privilege, and instead look for ways to justify or minimize the effects of privilege stating that their privilege was fully earned.** Typically, we justify privilege by acknowledging that some people are treated better than others and still deny that privilege is fully embedded in society. Some people who have privilege by virtue of race, gender, or national origin deny personally benefiting from it and may oppose dismantling it, in part because addressing privilege directly questions the assumption that society is a meritocracy (which it is not).

6. **Understand that there may be white individuals who are not wealthy or who do not have access to resources based on their socio-economic standing.** But it's important to know they wield privilege (and power) based on their skin color which is the overall defining baseline in Western society. There are advantages that are conferred and not earned. Advantages such as respect, the benefit of the doubt, and much more.

7. **Educate yourself and others by acknowledging that everyone in our society has been exposed to "the poison of racism" and white privilege.** Regardless of your race, racism is harmful to all of us. Racism doesn't just oppress non-whites, it oppresses *all* of us because it robs us of an equal, diverse, and loving society. If these statements make you uncomfortable, continue to discuss, read, and learn. Learning about the poison of racism is one specific way to help people make meaningful change in their awareness of how they perpetuate racism.

8. **Learn to listen.** Unearned privilege means that those who possess it are used to having their voices amplified. Actively listening to others and helping to amplify their voice will enable and empower others.

9. **Be aware that anger is real and exists in communities of color.** Listening and validating the anger of African American people, Indigenous people, and other people of color is a major step in ending white privilege. All of us need to take responsibility for doing our part to recognize our privilege and work to make the world more equitable.

See also: **Chapter 13:** Understanding Diversity of Race and Ethnicity

Chapter 19: Understanding Diversity of Poverty and Wealth Inequality

Chapter 22: Intersectionality

Chapter 22.
Intersectionality

In 1989, law professor and scholar Kimberlé Williams Crenshaw created the term *intersectionality* to capture that individuals' social identities (e.g., race, class, gender, gender identity, sexual orientation, religion, disability, physical appearance, age, and height) are not independent of one another and that individuals may experience "multiple oppressions" when disadvantaged identities overlap. Further, the impact of intersectionality is not limited to individuals who identify with groups that have been historically discriminated against. Intersectionality reminds us that we are all interconnected. Interconnectedness reminds us that we all should care.

1. **Intersectionality is more than an apolitical categorization of individuals' characteristics.** It goes beyond identity alone to emphasize the additive nature of oppressions as well as the political nature of combinations of identities.

2. **When applying intersectionality to the concept of privilege**, it can be understood as the way one form of privilege can be mitigated by other areas in which a person lacks privilege; for example, an African-American man has male privilege but no white privilege. Further, it rejects the concept of treating oppressive factors in isolation, as if discrimination against Asian women can be explained simply as a sum of discrimination against Asians + discrimination against women.

3. **Identify and make a list of your own various social identities.** How do you think each is perceived by those in your community? What about when you combine two or more? What is the impact on you, your work environment, family and friends?

4. **Make movie night revolve around a film or documentary that has a theme or storyline related to racism or discrimination** based on more than one aspect of a character. Discuss with others what the film meant to you. Do you think the character would have been treated differently if one or more of their characteristics were different? Similarly, you can examine real-life situations to consider how circumstances would be different for individuals with different intersections of identities. For example, if you see a white man and a white woman arguing on the street, consider how the situation could be seen differently if one or both of the people were a person of color, or gay, or disabled. What can you learn from these hypothetical situations about how you interpret what is happening and make assumptions?

5. **While many people claim to be allies for those who are marginalized, strive to be an advocate instead.** Directly involve yourself by affecting change whenever it's needed. For example, you can interrupt offensive or distasteful jokes or disrupt a heated argument.

6. **Learn to recognize examples of oppression in everyday life.** The urge to abuse power has often long-been a part of the human fabric of interaction from fascists and tyrants to ruthless executives, abusive parents, and schoolyard bullies; the systematic abuse of power is aided by social expectations of the worth of individuals based on their race, gender, etc.

7. **Exercise cultural relativism,** examining other cultures from their context. This means you have to do some work to understand others' contexts. You can start by reading books or listening to podcasts by individuals from different cultures to hear their perspectives.

See also: **Chapter 5:** How do I Define Myself?

Chapter 21: Privilege

Chapter 25: Being an Ally and an Advocate

Chapter 23.
A guide to -isms

The "-isms" refer to ways of understanding the world, whether positive or negative. They can be casual or systematic, and they can wreak havoc on our communities.

1. **Racism** includes prejudiced thoughts and discriminatory actions based on a difference in race/ethnicity and presumed superiority because of race. Since racism involves the use of power to isolate, separate, or exploit others, racism is usually perpetuated by people of white/European descent groups against persons of color. "Reverse racism" e.g., people of color not liking white people, isn't a thing because there's no component of power over the other group. Racism confers certain privileges on and defends the dominant group, which in turn, sustains and perpetuates racism.

2. **Sexism** is the prejudices and discrimination towards a person based on their sex or gender. This includes the belief that one sex is superior or of higher value than the other. An example of this is a woman receiving derogatory comments for continuing her career instead of being the main caretaker of her children. On the other side is an example of a man receiving derogatory comments for taking on the primary caretaker role for his children. Sexism can be insidious and systemic, such as women being skipped over for promotions because they had a child or because they *might* have a child; assumptions about loss of work time due to maternity leave and mothering often rely on women's higher burden of childrearing and perpetuate a system that discriminates against women.

3. **Heterosexism (homophobia)** is a range of negative attitudes, feelings, and behaviors toward homosexuality or people

who identify as LGBTQ. It has been defined as contempt, prejudice, aversion, hatred, or antipathy. It is often based on irrational fear and ignorance and related to religious beliefs. It is referred to as homophobia by combining *homo*sexual with *-phobia*, meaning "fear" or "aversion." The extreme forms of homophobia have resulted in several countries criminalizing homosexuality with imprisonment, torture, fines, or the death penalty. Homophobia contributed to the refusal to take the HIV/AIDS epidemic seriously when it first started.

4. **Ageism** is stereotyping and/or discrimination against individuals or groups on the basis of their age, usually referring to older individuals. Indeed, U.S. federal law describes age discrimination as discrimination against individuals 40 years or older because of their age. This can be combated by having younger generations connect with older generations to dispel the stereotypes of the generational gap. It helps change the youths' perspective about aging and shifts their respect for older generations by gaining insights and knowledge at a personal level.

5. **Adultism** is a new term referring to prejudiced thoughts and discriminatory actions against young people in favor of older people. Young people have opinions and perspectives that matter and should be valued as much as older people. Adults can do their part to listen and respect the voices of the youth.

6. **Ableism** is the belief that people with a disability are inferior to individuals without a disability, leading to discrimination toward and oppression of individuals with disabilities or physical differences. It can take many different forms such as buildings being constructed in a way that are inaccessible to people with physical disabilities, or assuming people with disabilities need to be 'fixed.'

7. **Classism** is prejudiced thoughts or discriminatory actions based on difference in income, socioeconomic status, or class, usually by upper classes against lower classes. This can lead to

superiority feelings if you're in a higher class or status than someone else. It divides people at the community and societal levels and deepen bitterness between the different classes.

8. **Colorism** is a form of prejudice where people are treated differently based on the social meanings attached to their skin color. For example, light-skinned African-Americans can be treated differently than darker-skinned African-Americans. Colorism can happen by members of the community itself and by individuals outside the community.

9. **Feminism** is the advocacy of women's rights on the grounds of the equality of the sexes. Feminism does not mean anti-men. It is the belief that men and women should have social, political, and economic equality. Feminism is standing up for inequalities women encounter in their daily lives.

10. **Xenophobia** isn't technically an "ism" but it is in a similar category: it is the fear or hatred of foreigners or strangers or of their culture. It can result in hostility towards someone who is considered an "outsider" or from a different background. Xenophobia can include acts of discrimination and/or violence towards immigrants, for example.

See also: **Chapter 7:** Stereotypes

Chapter 8: My Worldview

Chapter 26: Pre-judgements and Prejudices

Part 4:
Making Our Way in the World

Chapter 24.
Being Mindful

When we think of mindfulness, we usually think of meditation. But when it comes to diversity and inclusion, mindfulness means being conscious and aware of the cultural norms and cues in your organization and how those cultural norms and cues affect the mission of the company and your success as an employee. It's up to you to take inventory of your environment as well as your own values, beliefs and how you perceive others.

1. **Be mindful of addressing people who are different from you with the same level of respect that you would if they were a part of your inner circle.** How do you communicate with others who are culturally different? Oftentimes we can be condescending without even realizing it. Ask trusted friends to observe how you interact with others.

2. **Try to describe the world as closely as possible to how others see it.** This doesn't mean that you're trying to communicate as someone who you are not. It does mean, however, that you are seeking to operate from a place of cultural relativism. Always be mindful to ask questions if you're uncertain.

3. **Be mindful and encourage culturally diverse people to express themselves in their own uniqueness.** This might involve encouraging them to acknowledge Black History Month, ADHD Awareness Month or any of the countless other commemorations celebrating the uniqueness of people.

4. **Bring awareness into your communication with others whether at work or with friends.** Be mindful of your language and how it impacts others. It's important to use words that foster inclusion and acceptance.

5. **Have an attitude of curiosity, non-judgment, and kindness.** It helps to be mindful about our attitude and check-in on a daily basis. You will start to notice patterns when you are judgmental towards yourself or others and give yourself compassion in this process.

6. **Pay attention and listen to what others are saying and how they are acting.** By observing others and being fully present when you're having a conversation can open your eyes to understanding others more fully.

7. **Start with the intention to be more mindful.** It's impossible to be mindful 24/7, but just having the intention to incorporate it into your daily life will help shift your perspective. It can become a practice that you do more regularly and can be curious with.

8. **Being mindful helps create a welcoming environment.** It can be used as a tool for shifting perspectives and becoming more creative. It can create an inspiring workplace, homelife, etc.

See also: **Chapter 4:** What are My Values?

Chapter 27: Intentional Communication

Chapter 28: What is My Body Saying?

Chapter 25.
Being an Ally and an Advocate

Being an ally is being a collaborator who fights injustice and promotes equity through supportive personal relationships and acts of advocacy. Being an advocate goes even further and actively solicits others to join the cause, increase awareness, and engage hearts and minds. To become an ally and an advocate for diversity, equity, and inclusion, read on…

1. **The first step to becoming an ally is to do your homework.** Don't rely on people from underrepresented groups to educate you, as that's an unfair burden on them. Allies should make time to read, listen, watch, and deepen their understanding.

2. **If doing your homework seems exhausting, we understand.** To be fair, that is an experience many people have when they first start delving into this work. It's also fair to acknowledge that for most people in the world, they don't have the choice to learn about sexism, racism, homophobia and so on because it is an everyday aspect of their life. It's important to recognize that it is a privilege to have the opportunity to learn about oppression at your own pace and from relative safety.

3. **When you want to ask people about their experiences, ask their permission first.** Many women, people of color, and people from underrepresented groups have some psychic armor that they wear to protect them from everyday indignities. Ask permission before you ask someone to be vulnerable.

4. **Approach kindly with humility and curiosity.** For example, after you ask permission, you could ask, "I'm curious about

what challenges women/people of color/etc. experience in this workplace. Could you share things that might be difficult for you that I might not notice?" Recognize that not all women/people of color/etc. will have the same experience.

5. **Pay attention to how other groups experience gatherings.** You may not realize the extent to which people are uncomfortable or not heard or minimized. For example, many of us experience having our contribution to a group be ignored but then when someone else makes the same point, it is praised. Consider how it might or might not be helpful to speak up. Ask the individual if you're not sure how best you can support them.

6. **Recognize your own privilege.** To be an ally, it's important to recognize your own advantages and privilege and that others have been denied these same advantages and privileges. This is difficult for many people, because it means that the world is not merit-based and that you didn't completely earn all of your success. It can also be a source of shame for people, especially people who experienced less-visible adversity (such as childhood trauma) that they may still be processing. Shame makes it difficult to clearly see and accept privilege. In order to help others, it's important to recognize where they're coming from.

7. **... and use your privilege for good.** You can use your privilege as a white person or as a man (or many other identities that have privilege) to stand up for others who are not sure they will be heard and respected in the same way.

8. **When you see a problem, speak up.** Monitor your community and your workplace for racism, sexism, and homophobia, and speak up. Even if all you say is, "I'm not comfortable with this discussion," that's a step forward.

9. **Move into advocacy by becoming involved in movements to support policy change.** These activities can include participating in public protests or public celebrations of

diversity, phone banking for supportive candidates for office, or contributing funds or time to pro-diversity causes.

See also: **Chapter 21:** Privilege

Chapter 27: Intentional Communication

Chapter 44: Leveraging your Power to improve Diversity, Equity, and Inclusion

Chapter 26.
Pre-judgments and Prejudices

Let's get into a bit more detail about pre-judgements and prejudices. We just finished saying how important it is that we make every attempt possible to place ourselves in the shoes of the other person. This process, called cultural relativism, is how we fight the pre-judgments and prejudices that each of us hold. Prejudice occurs when we form opinions about a group of people based on little or no factual evidence. There are five ascending levels of prejudice which will be discussed below.

1. **The first, and seemingly harmless level, is** *antilocution.* Antilocution is a type of hate speech that targets another group. Ethnic jokes and declarative statements such as "The homeless are lazy people wo don't want to work" are examples of antilocution which sets the stage for more extreme forms of prejudice. If you heard someone making an ethnic joke at your job, how would you handle it? What if it was your boss?

2. **The second level of prejudice is** *avoidance.* This is when people avoid contact with members of the other group. If one of your co-workers on your team tried to avoid interacting with a member of a different group—even though the group member had access to very valuable information and you knew would be an asset to your project, what would you do?

3. **The next level prejudice is called** *discrimination.* This is when the person who is prejudiced attempts to exclude all members of the disliked group from access to services or resources. This can include employment, education, housing, and much more. Discrimination prevents access to opportunities and rights that belong to everyone.

4. *Physical violence* **is the next level.** Often we think of physical violence as attacks on our actual body. But physical violence

includes attacks on property as well. Anti-Semitic and racist slogans on locked room doors and ropes tied as nooses left on desks are examples of physical violence. It is important that you speak up and act well before things get to this stage at your workplace.

5. **The last and most extreme level of prejudice is *extermination* or *genocide*.** The physical violence has the objective of removing or eliminating all or major segments of the targeted group. While we may not see systemic prejudice carried out to this extreme in the workplace, it is important that we understand that allowing the levels to go unchecked can lead to behavior which condones and supports the most extreme form of prejudice.

6. **The best way to fight prejudice is intergroup contact and dialogue.** If management doesn't wish to invest in formalized diversity training to combat prejudice in the workplace, do you feel comfortable modeling behavior that is conducive to breaking down barriers? Would you call yourself an ally or an advocate for members of minority groups which are disenfranchised? If you are a part of a minority group, how would you address any of the above levels of prejudice if displayed at your workplace?

7. **Social media is a tool that can be positive or negative toward fighting prejudice.** It's what you do with it. As an employee be careful with what you post on your personal page. Things that we think are seen only by our friends have the potential to be seen by management and Human Resources. Companies are beginning to care more and more about how their employees are perceived outside of the company as well as when on duty with the company.

See also: **Chapter 6:** I'm Not Biased! (Am I?)

Chapter 12: What is Inclusion?

Chapter 23: A guide to -isms

Chapter 27.
Intentional Communication

Many of us speak and communicate without giving it a second thought. Although that tends to work out pretty well with people we know, who know us, and who have similar values, it's useful for communication with diverse populations to be more intentional. Here are some tips on how to think about what you say to intentionally promote diversity, equity, and inclusion.

1. **Communication can lead to conflict when we arrive with our perceptions while failing to acknowledge that our perceptions are always never entirely accurate.** Remember, we form our own reality based upon what we see, and we can never fully see the entire picture. This leads to conflicts in communication where the message, unlike on the commercial, is not heard.

2. **The most basic way for us to connect is through communication.** This is the fundamental method of interaction between individuals. Communication enables us to share ideas and feelings with one another. Communication can be verbal (such as saying "I like your hat") nonverbal (pointing to the hat and giving a thumbs up) or both (giving a thumbs up and saying you like the hat).

3. **Communication always begins with a source—a person.** The initiator who has an idea, message, feeling, thought, experience or anything else that they wish to share with someone else. Keep in mind that even if you're the source of the message, you're also the receiver. Think about a time when you were expressing your thoughts to someone. In addition to expressing your thoughts, what else were you doing? It is likely you were observing the other person and how they were responding to what was being said.

4. **When communicating, it's important to remember that we show respect for others.** Showing respect means treating people who may be different the way you wish to be treated. Snide remarks or casting "shade" does not exemplify respect for others. Have you ever been disrespected simply for being who you are? How did you feel?

5. **When connecting with others, understand that there will be differences.** True connection will embrace similarities and respect differences. It is up to us to remember that common ground is attainable if we reach for it. It is this common ground that will enable you to succeed as a team.

6. **Learn to accept responsibility for your behavior.** All of us fumble every now and then. We may say the wrong thing or make the wrong assumptions when it comes to people who are different than we are. The important thing is that we pick the ball up once it's dropped. And then we must make sure that once we pick the ball up, that it's handled properly. Remember, connecting and communicating are key!

7. **Remember for every action there is a reaction.** This is true when you connect with others in your workplace and beyond. When you connect with others, expect there to be a response. While you can't ultimately control the response of the other person, you can certainly have a great impact by thinking through your communication and how you connect with others who are different.

8. **One huge misstep when it comes to connecting and communicating is our tendency to generalize.** It's important to approach each individual and each situation from an objective point of view. This is called cultural relativism. It's when we attempt to place ourselves in the shoes of the other person and see the world from their point of view rather than our own.

9. **Remember that connecting and communicating with others allows you to send both verbal and nonverbal messages that**

shape the behavior of others. Because your communication has the power to shape others, you have the power to affect change in the culture.

10. **Be aware of code-switching by you or by others.** This is when members of a particular group automatically adjust their language and vernacular to fit in with those in the mainstream. Code-switching is done not to hide one's identity. For many, it has become part of a natural behavior enabling the person to assimilate into the working environment. For example, many of us speak in a "professional" tone when we are at work, and in a less formal vernacular when we are at home with our families. Code-switching can also be done in many non-work circumstances, including among friends and family and in different neighborhoods. Are there ways in which you code-switch? What can you learn from observing your own code-switching and that of others?

See also: **Chapter 24:** Being Mindful

Chapter 28: What is My Body Saying?

Chapter 29: How to Apologize and Mean it

Chapter 28.
What Is My Body Saying?

Ralph Waldo Emerson once famously said, "What you do speaks so loudly that I cannot hear what you say." In this chapter, we will deal specifically with what we say with our bodies. We communicate with others using verbal (using words and sounds) and nonverbal (gestures, facial expressions or other body language) messages. Research demonstrates that when our verbal and nonverbal messaging conflicts, the recipient is more likely to believe our nonverbal communication over our verbal communication. Therefore, it is advantageous for us to pay attention to what our bodies are saying even though our mouths may be saying something entirely different.

1. **Nonverbal communication is also referred to as nonverbal cues because they "cue" us in on the real feelings of the person despite the verbal message that is being conveyed.** Cues can include nuances of one's voice, body movement and the body's orientation toward others, facial expressions, and gestures. Even how one might relate to objects — an obsessive tapping of a pencil on one's desk, for instance — is likely indicative of emotions or feelings other than what is said verbally.

2. **It is very important to always remember that how others see and perceive you will impact your success in achieving your goals, whether those are to be kind to others, to be a respectful part of your community or to achieve goals at work.** While no one is encouraging you to act phony, you should certainly be aware of what you're doing. Other aspects of how we present ourselves, such as how we dress, how we style our hair, and whether we wear jewelry, all give others information that they then interpret according to their own assumptions and prejudices.

3. **Learn about differences in nonverbal communication. For example, in some cultures, it's rude to make direct eye contact.** This is particularly true in relationships where there is a hierarchy. It is disrespectful in these cultures for a subordinate to directly speak to someone while looking intently into their eyes. In Western culture (the North American continent and Western Europe), if you do not look someone in the eye it can be interpreted as a sign of weakness or deception.

4. **Handshakes, like eye contact, vary from culture to culture.** While this book is being written, the world is experiencing a pandemic. Handshakes and other greetings and behaviors are being reexamined. Some cultures a kiss on the cheek (for both women and men) has been acceptable or even expected as a greeting in business settings. This is all changing. It would do the young professional good to continue to be apprised about the best way to greet colleagues and clients in light of changing norms.

5. **Touching is also an area of cultural sensitivity.** Some cultures greet each other with kisses on each cheek; in other cultures, including the U.S., it would generally be considered offensive if someone you didn't know leaned in for a kiss on the cheek. In the U.S., we generally don't touch people we don't know, but a conversation I (JPW) had with some friends in Brazil revealed they thought it bizarre that in the U.S. we are uncomfortable with strangers touching our kids; in Brazil it was normal for a stranger to pat a child on the head or touch them on the shoulder, and they thought it odd that North Americans were so standoffish.

6. **Nonverbal messaging also includes how we use our time.** This is especially important in the workplace because people from different cultures view time differently. For example, some cultures take a very flexible view of time, where "let's meet at 8" could mean meeting anywhere between 8:30 and 10. For people who view time as much more rigid, this

could be interpreted that the other person doesn't care or is unprofessional.

See also: **Chapter 24:** Being Mindful

Chapter 27: Intentional Communication

Chapter 35: Navigating the Multicultural Workplace

Chapter 29.
How to Apologize and Mean it

Sometimes we all say something insensitive or uncaring. The thing to do when we mess up is to apologize and to promise to do better. Not sure how to broach this difficult topic? We can help!

1. **Recognize that you messed up.** This involves a lot of the previous work in recognizing privilege, being sensitive to others' feelings, and being aware of how our words and actions (and inaction) affect others. Until you're aware something is wrong, it's hard to fix it.

2. **Feel remorse.** There's no skipping this step. If you don't actually feel badly for what you did or said, your apology will come across as hollow.

3. **Admit responsibility.** No sneaking across this line with "I'm sorry you feel hurt" or "Mistakes were made." Those are lame and not actually taking responsibility for your actions. Step up and say what you did and that you take responsibility. Examples: "I'm sorry I didn't stand up for you when Sal was picking on you. I should have." Or "I'm sorry I used that word. I didn't realize how it would come across and I should have."

4. **Remember, it's about their experience, not your intent.** People can feel hurt, humiliated, or embarrassed whether you intended it or not. This is a really important aspect to internalize. Even when we hurt people accidentally, they are still hurt, and we should still apologize. If you have any doubt on this one, please talk to other people until you truly understand. Apologize when your action (or inaction) hurts other people.

5. **Eliminate excuses.** If you said something rude or offensive, own it. Don't bother saying, "I don't usually say that around other people" or "I never use that word" or "I didn't know it would affect you." Those are excuses, and they are not helpful to anyone. Take responsibility for not knowing, because we should know how to communicate without offending people. The proper response is not to say, "I didn't know" but "I should have known."

6. **Promise it won't happen again.** Tell the person it won't happen again, and – this is really important – make sure it doesn't happen again. Apologies are worthless if they don't also involve a change in behavior.

7. **Listen.** The other person gets to have their experience regardless of how you might feel. Your apology does not obligate them to forgive and forget, and sometimes an apology doesn't erase the hurt, embarrassment, or humiliation someone feels. Listen and give them space. They don't owe you anything.

8. **Put it all together and learn from the experience**. Apologies are an important way to show you respect and value others. And that you respect and value yourself. When you know better, do better.

See also: **Chapter 21:** Privilege

Chapter 24: Being Mindful

Chapter 27: Intentional Communication

Part 5:
How to Change the World

Part 5:
How to Change the World

Chapter 30.
Building Belonging

People are naturally social creatures. Even those of us who are introverts acknowledge that a sense of belonging is essential. Whether it is a feeling of belonging in your immediate family, your neighborhood, a social organization or on your job, we need a sense of kinship with others if we are going to effectively engage and meet our goals — both personal and professional. Studies show that people tend to gravitate and feel a sense of belonging with those who they most identify. But in the workplace, it's important to remember that everyone 'belongs'. This is what it means to be inclusive and not just diverse. But how can you help create a sense of belonging, especially if you're not in management.

1. **Advocate for others who are different or who may feel marginalized because of their identity.** It's easy to be silent, but it's much more challenging and advantageous to suggest that the hijab that your neighbor or co-worker wears is not a disturbance or distraction as some may claim. You can speak up and let others know how important it is that she is comfortable in her attire so that she can feel like she belongs. As a result, she will perform better. Everybody wins.

2. **Suggest that the company start affinity groups (also known as employee resource groups.)** Affinity groups bring people from within the company with shared interests. It's a great way for employees to know that the company cares about them holistically and not just what they do while sitting at their desk during the day.

3. **Present management with a few statistics.** Management loves to know how the bottom line of the company will be affected by new initiatives. Studies show that employees with

a high sense of belonging take 75% fewer sick days than those who feel as if they're excluded. Employees also have a 50% higher turnover rate when they feel excluded, and they are 25% less productive in working toward the goals of their team. Those are important numbers for management to pay attention to!

4. **Be intentional about cultivating relationships with people who are not like you.** You can make a list of individuals you come in contact with and be deliberate about speaking to them or even asking them out to lunch. Regularly journal how your interactions turned out. Were they positive or negative? Why do you think they turned out the way they did? What did you learn about the other person? What did you learn about yourself?

5. **When people feel isolated, they lose a sense of purpose.** It's important that you, along with your co-workers, eradicate isolation and replace it with intentional actions designed to let others know that they are valued and that they belong to the team.

6. **Consider online organization or public communities.** These communities can include your company's internal Slack, Jabber, or Google instant messaging services, or public Twitter, LinkedIn, Instagram, or other social media to connect with others. Reach out and build relationships!

7. **Consider a formal or informal mentorship.** Often new people who are struggling to belong are looking for a one-on-one relationship where they can gradually get to know the company and others.

See also: **Chapter 12:** What is Inclusion?

Chapter 10: Why Diversity Matters

Chapter 25: Being an Ally and an Advocate

Chapter 31.
Building Bridges

Bridges are important. Think about the last time you crossed a long bridge. Each year when I (LDJ) drive to Hampton, Virginia, for a conference, I have to cross the Chesapeake Bay Bridge, which has two spans totaling more than 8.5 miles of a narrow structure with low guardrails. It often sits very close to the water, and in high winds it sways in a terrifying way. Needless to say, for me, it is not the most relaxing part of my trip. However, it is a very necessary part of my trip, and without that bridge, I would never arrive at my destination. We too must build bridges to arrive at our common destination — no matter how uncomfortable or challenging the task may be.

1. **The best way to build bridges with others is to become informed.** Too often we are eager to connect. But to do so without taking the time to learn more about others will result in more isolation and will create more of a gulf than a bridge. The internet is a fantastic way to find out about other cultures. But an even better way is to simply strike up a dialogue with others. You will find that discussing differences does not have the same stigma that it did many decades ago.

2. **Partner with someone who is different with the intention of facilitating positive and diverse change in your community or company.** The two of you can become ambassadors and build bridges of inclusion.

3. **Know that when you build bridges of inclusion, you're building bridges of opportunities.** These opportunities are not just for others, but when you become a bridge builder, you will find that you are stretched to know more and to do more. It's definitely a win-win situation!

4. **When you set out to be a bridge-builder, you may not see the destination.** The Chesapeake Bay Bridge was so frightening because I couldn't see the other end from my windshield. It may appear that you are at risk at drowning in a sea of indifference and unfamiliarity, but stay on course. The journey is worth the effort!

5. **One of the best things that you can do when building bridges in the workplace is to listen.** To everyone! Even the difficult people. Especially the difficult people who often encourage cultural division. Find out why they're against cultural diversity and inclusion. Often the answers are not what we may think.

6. **Talk a lot to a lot of people.** Well, not during business hours when you're supposed to be working! But talk a lot about other people — good things, of course! Think of positive things to say about others who are different. Positive-speak goes a long way!

See also: **Chapter 12:** What is Inclusion?

Chapter 38: Building the Multicultural Workplace

Chapter 44: Leveraging your Power to improve Diversity, Equity, and Inclusion

Chapter 32.
Communicating for Change

Often everyday communication can be difficult and challenging, even with family and close friends. Imagine communicating with diverse individuals in the workplace! All sorts of misunderstandings are likely to occur. However, for any real change to occur—whether it is a change in the direction of the company or a change in how individuals will be recognized and respected—there first must be mutual understanding. Communication can be defined as the imparting or interchange of thoughts, opinions, or information by speech, writing, or signs. It helps create identities, and assists in gathering information about others, which allows you to influence other people. Hopefully in a positive way!

1. **Interpersonal communication involves the exchange of information, ideas, and feelings between people through verbal or nonverbal means.** Of course, what we intend and what is received are not always completely in alignment. With people who are different from us (e.g., race, country of origin, gender), we may have to work harder to be fully understood. For example, think of the last time you were misunderstood by someone. How did you feel? What could you have done differently to be a bridge builder for understanding in that situation?

2. **When communicating for change -- whether it's company-wide or whether you wish to address a conflict with a co-worker -- begin with a goal in mind.** Determining your goal will give you a clearer path toward helping the other person understand what you want to convey. Think of ways that can help you determine your goal. Perhaps you can write it down on a sheet of paper. Or maybe you can record it on your mobile device and play it back. Perhaps you can post it on a sticky and keep it somewhere visible. What works best for you?

3. **If you feel uncomfortable talking face-to-face with your co-worker, you can send an email or a note.** Keep in mind, that in some cultures, important topics should be discussed in person. Make sure that you understand what is best for your moment of interpersonal communication.

4. **When attempting to make a change with a wider audience, you can use social media.** Start a private Facebook group for your company or department. Invite individuals from diverse backgrounds to participate. Many people welcome the ability to participate through social media rather than in person. Communicating about intense topics, including many issues of diversity, equity, and inclusion, are best done via other means.

5. **Think about starting an online newsletter or other kind of update.** This can be done in partnership with someone else whose background is different from yours. You can highlight the achievements of others. Demonstrating the accomplishments of others is a great way to change the culture in a positive way.

6. **Listening is an important part of communicating.** If the goal is to truly understand each other, you'll need to do some listening too. Ask questions if you don't understand. Go easy on your own anecdotes and comparisons. In order to be understood, seek to understand.

7. **Work on transparency as much as possible within the boundaries of appropriate cultural communication.** Americans typically communicate directly, verbally, assertively, and persuasively in their speech. When working with a more diverse group, however, it's important to respect other methods of communication. And of course, pay attention to the nonverbal communication – the person you're communicating with probably is!

See also: **Chapter 27:** Intentional Communication

Chapter 28: What is My Body Saying?

Chapter 33: Communicating for Growth

Chapter 33.
Communicating for Growth

Now that we've discussed communicating for change, we can be a bit more specific and address communication for growth. Your development as an individual as well as that of your team and the company, is important. If you're not growing, then you're stagnant. And stagnation is never good. In fact, it's toxic.

1. **Remember when we said that before you even begin the communication process with another person, that you should have a goal in mind?** Well, the same thing applies to when you're communicating for change within your organization. Perhaps even more so because you are not just attempting to influence one individual. Rather you're attempting to sway entire groups of people toward a trajectory of growth.

2. **How did you feel when you realized that someone was being deceptive?** Pretty bad, I'm sure. That's why transparency is very important when you are communicating with a goal of growth in mind. Studies show that less than a quarter of American workers say that they have full insight into how their organization is doing. They believe that the company is holding something back. What can you do to be more transparent? Can you encourage others, particularly those at the top of the job chain, to be more transparent?

3. **Often we say that we want growth, but we do not have a growth mindset.** Before you can communicate change, you must think and believe that change is possible. There's no use in waking up in the morning and dreading going to work. It's important to adopt and maintain a positive mindset. Think of

ways you can be positive even when discouraging situations arise.

4. **Make sure that you're actively listening.** It can be easy to become so eager to affect change in your environment that you forget to practice listening to others. Remember, listening is not just done with your ears. It's done with your heart.

5. **Include everyone.** Sometimes we leave people out if we feel they may not be interested or if they have a reputation for being difficult. But if you're going to communicate for growth, it's important to include every person who is on your team.

6. **Clarify your expectations of others.** Do not assume that people know what you mean. Be clear and ask the other person to repeat back to you what they heard you say.

7. **Host or suggest a training session.** Training sessions are great because they're often mandatory and also because the platform for communicating growth is one that can be viewed as "official."

8. **Use visuals.** Signs are a great way to communicate change and growth in your organization. If you're using images of people on your visuals, make sure that they reflect a diverse population — this is important even if your company is not yet diverse. You are communicating an important change that is to be realized for the growth of the company.

See also: **Chapter 12:** What is Inclusion?

Chapter 27: Intentional Communication

Chapter 28: What is My Body Saying?

Chapter 34.
Managing Discussion Disasters

Imagine you have new colleague from the Middle East who has been doing extremely well on your team. You pass them in the hallway and give a quick thumbs up. The next day your colleague refuses to speak to you. In order to get work done and be productive you and your colleague must interact. What happened? What's your next move? After a bit of internet research, you find out that in certain Middle Eastern countries giving someone the thumbs up is the equivalent of giving someone the middle finger in the U.S.! Without even saying a word, any subsequent discussions have already been curtailed. Now that you're aware, you can avoid a *discussion disaster* and can explain the cultural difference to your colleague and let them know just how excited you are that they are a part of the team. Because of cultural differences, what may be a simple discussion might turn in to a disaster because of differences. Let's look at a few differences and see how we can bridge the cultural gap between people with different backgrounds, experiences, and perspectives.

1. **"Silence is sometimes the answer."** This Estonian proverb points to a specific response you or others can make when things go wrong. Remember that the messages you send — both verbal and nonverbal— and the responses they produce are rooted in culture.

2. **Remember, language is a set of shared symbols or signs (verbal and written) that a group of people have mutually agreed to use to help create meaning.** When someone new enters the group there is always the possibility of a *discussion disaster*. Develop a plan of action which includes a communication strategy that will let newcomers know that you care, even if you may get "it" wrong every now and then.

3. **Beware of colleagues who use microaggressions by "jokingly" imitating the accent of someone else.** Microaggressions are commonplace verbal, behavioral, or environmental indignities – either intentional or unintentional – that communicate hostile slights to people of another group. Such jokes are symptomatic of unconscious bias and can have a detrimental effect on your team and impede the communication necessary for productivity. Do not be afraid to take your colleague to the side and advise them about the negative impact their "humor" can have on the team.

4. **Practice being mindful when communicating with others who are culturally different.** This might mean that you are receptive to new information, realizing that others may not share your perspective. Remember if the other person's first language is not the same as yours and the majority of others in your organization, that they will experience greater pressure along with greater cognitive demands.

5. **Make it a habit to employ the practice of "checking" during your intercultural conversations.** This means that if the other person has difficulty comprehending because their native language is not the same as yours, you can offer to rephrase your comment or question. Be careful not ask questions that place the responsibility of understanding on the other individual. For example, you might ask "Am I clear?" Rather than "Do you understand?" In this way the responsibility and focus is on you and not the other individual.

6. **Consider ground rules for teams.** If you're communicating as part of a team and keep running into disasters, consider clarifying some ground rules to which everyone can agree. These can include, "One person talks at a time," "Respectful communication only," and "Everyone gets to contribute."

7. **If anyone is egregiously or persistently being disrespectful (including racist, sexist, homophobic, or otherwise), they**

may be breaking the law. Consider discussing with your boss, Human Resources (which is there to protect the organization), or a lawyer (who is there to protect you) if disrespectful language or actions do not stop.

See also: **Chapter 26:** Pre-judgements and Prejudices

Chapter 27: Intentional Communication

Chapter 35: Navigating the Multicultural Workplace

Chapter 35.
Navigating the Multicultural Workplace

On a recent Delta Airlines flight, I (LDJ) was mesmerized by the pre-flight video on the screen in front of me. The first words were, "The first step toward connection is departure." The video then began to show all of the new and wonderful countries I could visit and the many diverse communities I could experience. I had to buckle my seat belt and get ready for departure—and then I could connect to an amazing world full of diverse people! I was psyched! Prior to departing on the adventure, a pilot has to make sure that their navigation system is current and that it has been programmed with the right destination in mind. When navigating the multicultural workplace, we have to depart from our usual perspective in order to make the critical connection with others who may be different.

1. **Be deliberate with knowing how you are going to navigate a workspace that is either in need of diversity or that may be diverse but not inclusive.** With your workplace in mind (or if you're not working, think about your academic setting), how diverse is the context? Is it equitable? Is it inclusive? Once you have your answers, thinking of how someone who is of a different race, gender, sexual orientation, age, religion, or ability might answer those questions. Would they find the workplace context quite different than you do?

2. **Educate yourself.** There is an abundance of information available that can be helpful as you empower yourself and others to embrace diversity, equity and inclusion. This book is a great start! Also check out the recommended readings at the end of the book.

3. **Cultural relativism is when we view others' culture from their own perspective.** While this may be difficult at first based on our own biases and ethnocentrism, it is possible. Develop a habit of curiosity. Develop a habit of wondering what the other person might be thinking or feeling because they may be "different."

4. **Be intentional each day about how you are going to approach others.** You are aware that a diverse workplace may be uncomfortable for some. Envision possible scenarios and how you can be an effective agent of change.

5. **Learn from your workplace.** In addition to learning how comfortable you are around those who are unlike you or whether you feel more at ease with those who are from a similar background (racial, ethnic, sexual orientation, etc.), identify how your colleagues address these issues. Do you feel that there is an overall respect and acceptance for those who are different? When respect and acceptance for diversity are missing in the workplace, then there is room for conflict and disputes which lead to an unproductive work environment. Have you ever observed situations of conflict? Is conflict handled in an inclusive way? How diverse is the workforce, including the workers, managers, senior officials, and the board of directors? Some organizations have non-white and female individuals concentrated at lower-level positions.

6. **Realize that just because there is a diverse workplace, doesn't mean that inclusion and equity exist.** Individuals can be included but there may be no equity. And even in the rare times where diversity, equity and inclusion are achieved, we now realize that it doesn't not necessarily yield a sense of belonging.

7. **Sometimes people pretend that diversity, equity, and inclusion isn't "their problem."** Or they pretend to misunderstand rules in a hostile way (e.g., "It's no longer safe to talk to women at work, so I'm going to exclude them

from my team"). Are there ways you can learn from this behavior too?

See also: **Chapter 9:** What is Diversity?

Chapter 11: Equality vs. Equity

Chapter 12: What is Inclusion?

Chapter 36.
Be Adept at Adapting

Being adept at adapting means being effective at changing when a situation calls for change. Some people get stuck in their ways and see all change as negative. As the world is in constant change and motion, we all need to become better at adaptation in the workplace, homelife, relationships, and within our society.

1. **Let go of the "that's the way it's always been done" mentality.** If we stay stagnant in that mindset, it will be difficult to be open to change.

2. **Become more open-minded.** The more we embrace change and new situations the more likely we are to encourage others to be more open-minded.

3. **Learn about the new situation you may encounter.** Sometimes we get stuck in fears of other ways of living, eating, working, etc. When we face these fears, we allow ourselves to shift into a place where change can be embraced as a positive instead of a negative thing.

4. **Adaptability is a positive quality.** People who are able to adapt to change easily are more likely to focus on possibilities, be more curious, and have the ability to see opportunities and solutions when facing challenges. They are more likely to work well in a team or collaborative environment.

5. **Change will happen.** Once you can accept change will happen then it opens the possibility up for you to become more adaptable to it. We have the opportunity to decide how to respond to change and we can look at that as an empowering opportunity.

6. **Sometimes you need to take risks.** Maybe starting with something smaller and gradually increase. This will allow you to slowly become more adaptable to a new situation with ease.

7. **Learning is key.** When you learn about a new technology or a new way of doing something this helps you embrace adaptability. Learn from others to gain new insights whether it's through reading, seminars, podcasts, etc.

8. **Healthy tools are important when experiencing change.** Even if you are extremely adept at adapting, it can still be stressful. Too much stress can be unhealthy. It's important to have a balance and to incorporate lots of self-care tools when going through change whether small or big. If there's a lot of change happening at once it can be helpful to have one constant such as every morning running for 30 minutes.

See also: **Chapter 24:** Being Mindful

Chapter 35: Navigating the Multicultural Workplace

Chapter 37: Be the Change You Wish to See

Chapter 37.
Be the Change You Wish to See

If we want to see changes happen then we need to look at ourselves first. We need to start by setting an example and make changes in our own lives that we want to see reflected in our communities, societies, and in the world. We have to change ourselves first by shifting our mentality, habits, and actions.

1. **Self-evaluation** is an important process in order to make positive changes in ourselves. You can look at the areas within yourself you would like to change that also is reflected in the changes you want to see happen outside of yourself. This is a helpful process to become aware of habits we might not have even recognized before that we want to change.

2. **Become aware of self-talk and language you use towards others.** If you want to see more respect in your workplace check-in to see if you are being respectful in your own self-talk and in the language you use with your colleagues.

3. **Learn from others.** If you want to make changes in yourself it's helpful to research and learn about how others made changes in their lives and gain insights.

4. **Create habits that positively reinforce the change you wish to see in yourself and others.** Kindness is a habit that can be added into your daily life and it can start small and evolve from there.

5. **Step out of your comfort zone.** Many of us have adapted a daily routine that feels safe. Sometimes it is helpful to push that comfort zone to grow even as uncomfortable as it may feel. Traveling to another country definitely pushes us out of our daily comfort zone and it could have a positive impact on

your perspectives and maybe even the way you decide to live your life.

6. **Surround yourself with others who are aligned with the changes you wish to see.** When you are around a group of people who also want to change themselves for the better and make a positive impact it can help foster your own motivation and growth. You can learn from each other and have a built-in support system.

7. **Use social media platforms.** You can use social media for positive change. It can be a platform where you use your voice to share positive language, actions, events, knowledge, experiences, etc. Through social media you can connect with others who are also working towards change for the positive. Setting intentions before using these platforms is helpful to keep your focus on what you're using them for and not getting off-track.

8. **Take action and volunteer.** One of the best activities you can join in is by volunteering for something you truly believe in or wish to learn more about. It can connect you with a community that also want the changes you wish to see. It not only helps others, but it also helps yourself by changing your mindset and your view of others.

See also: **Chapter 1:** Who Am I?

      Chapter 27: Intentional Communication

      Chapter 36: Be Adept at Adapting

Part 6.
Leading to Promote Diversity, Equity, and Inclusion

Chapter 38.
Building the Multicultural Workplace

Diverse cultures are creative cultures. These diverse cultures poised to produce new and innovative ideas. However, just because diverse cultures are creative and poised to produce new ideas doesn't mean that those ideas are actually implemented. Studies show that despite the ability to be innovative, diverse cultures are not always inclusive cultures. When individuals feel excluded, they withhold ideas. It is important that individuals on your team are encouraged and are comfortable sharing.

1. **Consider who's being promoted in your organization, and how promotion decisions are made.** Are promotions given to those who request them? Those who speak up? Those who spend long hours in the office? If so, you might be holding back some people, including those with softer communication styles, family needs for flexible hours, or people who are more shy about speaking up.

2. **The key to equality in the workplace is looking at all scopes.** Even the most well-intentioned companies discover discrepancies between the equality they want and the equality that exists. Open yourself up to finding these inequalities so that you can you take steps to fix them

3. **Ensure that diverse members of your team are not assigned to menial tasks.** Diverse team members may feel overlooked or dismissed when given responsibilities that are unrewarding and mundane.

4. **Encourage your diverse teammates to take on challenges that reflect their skillset or that will enable them to learn new skills.** Show that you have already bought into their ability to contribute to the team and organization.

133

5. **Diversity pays off: a higher representation of women in C-Suite positions results in 34% greater returns to shareholders.** Likewise, African Americans who have made inroads at top positions have been able to prove their worth and value. Today, African Americans make up about 3% of high-level executives in major companies in the United States. However, the success of American Express and Lowes Home Improvement under focused leaders are testimonials that given the right environment, women and other minorities can make a huge difference in the bottom line of a company.

6. **Commit to advocating not just for diversity training, but equity and inclusion training so that awareness can be made about the importance of a diverse company.** Being culturally aware is just a beginning – it's equally important to be culturally competent. Without the equity and inclusion components of promoting and ensuring fairness and belonging, diversity training will likely fall flat.

7. **Ensure that co-workers have access to training and support that will enable them to build their skillset and morale and which will likely encourage them to share ideas and come up with creative solutions.** As above, move beyond training to ensure that there is visibility and support from leadership to face diversity, equity, and inclusion challenges and create solutions.

8. **Flexible work arrangements can be very beneficial to the development of a diverse and inclusive workforce.** Flexibility such as work-from-home options help to alleviate the pressures of recruiting diversity candidates who may be a good fit for a role but may not be in a position to relocate. Flexibility provides the added benefit of aiding in the recruitment and retention of women at the senior level who, despite working full-time, still take on the bulk of household and childcare responsibilities.

9. **Share stories in your organization and with the community about successful individuals** who are women, members of minority groups, part of the LGBTQ community, or who are disabled. Invite individuals and groups to share their own experiences.

See also: **Chapter 10:** Why Diversity Matters

Chapter 12: What is Inclusion?

Chapter 39: Setting Workplace Diversity Goals

Chapter 39.
Setting Workplace Diversity Goals

Diversity goals are often equated with setting quotas for hiring people who are not white and male; in reality, however, progress is about so much more than percentages. Diversity goals are about your organization's values, your employees' feedback, and the integration and inclusion of all employees and stakeholders into your organization's culture.

1. **Solicit team-wide input.** It's important to hear stories from employees, even if those stories are disturbing, about their problematic and positive experiences with your organization. This input can be in the form of quantitative surveys that include the degree of agreement or disagreement with statements like "My organization is a safe and inclusive place for me to work." It can also include interviews with individuals in the organization who would like to offer feedback on how people are treated and any challenges they've encountered.

2. **Ensure you have buy-in from the highest executives.** Leverage research and data that points to the value of diversity, equity, and inclusion in a healthy and successful workplace. Request that senior people make an appearance at trainings or events and say a few words demonstrating their support. Similarly, discuss with mid-level managers how to best be receptive to constructive feedback and complaints from employees about diversity issues without getting defensive.

3. **Measure bias.** Consider measuring unconscious bias by examining hiring processes and representation across the organization. This can include not just the diversity of individuals in your organization compared to the local community, but also who is represented on hiring committees,

as managers, and on the board of directors. You can send surveys to candidates about their hiring experience. You can also cross-reference the percentage of resumes moved forward to screening or interview with demographic data to identify where underrepresented groups may fall off the hiring process.

4. **Set SMART diversity, equity, and inclusion goals that have a variety of challenges and timelines.** SMART goals that are those that are specific, measurable, achievable, realistic, and time-bound (they have a deadline). Set some goals that may be easy to reach and others that are stretch goals, which require you to go beyond your comfort zone to work harder. Too many easy goals and you won't be challenged enough; too many stretch goals and you may get too discouraged. Finally, set goals that have a variety of timelines: some that can be achieved within weeks; others within a month or two; and big goals to be achieved within a year or two. Consider breaking big goals down into smaller chunks with shorter target dates for completion.

5. **Coordinate with Human Resources to ensure your initiatives are supported by strong policies and procedures.** Policies and procedures should address non-retaliation, retaining underrepresented talent, exit interviews, and employee advocacy. Training during onboarding and periodically throughout employees' tenure at the organization should reiterate the organization's strong support of diversity, equity, and inclusion.

6. **Address detractors directly and kindly.** Sometimes organizations experience backlash to diversity, equity, and inclusion initiatives; addressing these detractors in a way that acknowledges their concerns while also clarifying the organization's goals and values is key.

7. **Ensure accountability.** Own the initiatives and commit to transparency in the organization. Communicate about

progress – or lack thereof – and solicit input to ensure involvement.

See also: **Chapter 40:** Increasing Representation in the Pipeline

Chapter 41: Diversity in Recruitment and Hiring

Chapter 44: Leveraging your Power to improve Diversity, Equity, and Inclusion

Chapter 40.
Increasing Representation
in the Pipeline

We have heard many times from managers to C-suite leaders to government leaders, "We would have hired a [underrepresented person], but we just didn't know anyone!" This is a failure at many levels, because true diversity, equity, and inclusion isn't just putting a person with certain demographics in a leadership position; it's supporting diverse individuals throughout the entire pipeline from school to new employee to manager to senior leader.

1. **Recruit and broadcast opportunities widely.** Consider outreach activities to recruit at universities, represent the company at conferences, or recruit in organizations that include many people of color (such as specific sororities and fraternities) or many diverse people (such as LinkedIn). You can also use nontraditional recruiting platforms such as Jopwell (representing African American, Latinx, and Native American students and professionals), include.io, or community groups such as Lesbians who Tech, Vets who Code, and Black Girls Code. The more intentional you are about your determination to find the best people, the more it will become a part of your culture.

2. **Providing access to training opportunities for underrepresented groups** at lower levels in the organization will boost efforts to create a more diverse and inclusive senior leadership team by ensuring that diverse candidates are eligible and qualified for promotions. Find out what your employees need to know and provide both structured training opportunities.

3. **Establish mentorship programs** that specifically match senior individuals (of any demographic) with mentees from

underrepresented groups also offer employees a feeling of belonging and a safe place to discuss sensitive issues.

4. **Actual leadership opportunities provide a chance for junior people from underrepresented groups to learn from senior individuals.** These leadership opportunities could include being on a committee, co-leading a project, or participating in a "leadership internship" to shadow a senior member of the organization. Skill building is essential; building relationships and confidence is a bonus!

5. **Often the biggest barrier to building a diverse and inclusive workforce is the unfounded concern that an organization must sacrifice quality to meet a quota.** The truth is that high quality, diverse talent exists, but it may be harder to find because by definition there are fewer minority individuals than those in the majority. Clarify that your quality standards are not changing, and that you will provide equitable support to help all talented individuals succeed.

6. **Be proactive.** Companies should make a point to engage with diverse talent on an ongoing basis long before the need arises to pull new people into the organization. By proactively getting to know people of varying backgrounds, leaders will be prepared to hire diverse talent with speed and confidence.

See also: **Chapter 39:** Setting Workplace Diversity Goals

Chapter 41: Diversity in Recruitment and Hiring

Chapter 44: Leveraging your Power to improve Diversity, Equity, and Inclusion

Chapter 41.
Diversity in Recruitment and Hiring

Even if your organization is delighted to interview talented employees from underrepresented groups, it's possible the experience from their perspective is not as rosy. How do you focus on diversity in recruitment and hiring? Read on...

1. **Let's repeat: Often the biggest barrier to building a diverse and inclusive workforce is the unfounded concern that an organization must sacrifice quality to meet a quota.** The truth is that high quality, diverse talent exists, but it may be harder to find because by definition there are fewer minority individuals than those in the majority. Clarify that your quality standards are not changing, and that you will provide equitable support to help all talented individuals succeed at your company.

2. **Use creative search strings in your job ads.** For example, you can tag community groups such as Lesbians Who Tech, Hack the Hood, Vets Who Code, and so on. You could also add "she/her" as a search term.

3. **Acknowledge conscious and unconscious bias, prejudice, and values that may increase or decrease comfort of people from underrepresented groups.** Frequent and impactful training is helpful for hiring teams. Oversight and feedback from hiring committees is also helpful. For example, one of us (JPW) was on a hiring team where the chair of the committee, a senior white man, read a statement attesting to the organization's emphasis on diversity that chairs were required to read. Then, in full view of the committee, he tossed it on the floor and he said that we would make our own decisions. The effect was chilling on the rest of the committee.

4. **Pay attention to how people discuss candidates, as that can also reveal biases.** Consider whether evaluations are accurate; for example, someone who is quiet is not necessarily a poor leader and someone who is gregarious is not necessarily a good leader. Push yourselves to challenge each other's interpretations in respectful ways to ensure the best talent pool.

5. **Write clear and compelling job descriptions that focus on impact.** Focus your job descriptions on potential impact, what candidates are expected to know, and what candidates could learn on the job instead of a checklist of what characteristics/ skills the person should have. You can also identify if required qualifications, such as educational requirements, could be adjusted for people with comparable lived experience. This is especially important because men typically apply for a job when they meet only 60 percent of the qualifications, whereas women don't feel confident to apply unless they meet 100 percent.

6. **Train hiring teams to reach consensus on how candidates should be evaluated, how resumes should be reviewed, and how interviews should be conducted.** Identify, for example, whether teams should focus on accomplishments, growth, conscientiousness, or a combination of these. Focus on open-ended questions to help you understand how people approached a situation, not just what was completed.

7. **Develop relationships between recruiters, hiring managers, and human resources staff.** Transparency and communication are key to understanding biases and stereotypes and insisting on reviewing a variety of candidates to find the right one to be successful in your organization.

8. **Commit to fair compensation.** Document your current compensation process, including salary ranges, what's negotiable, and how those negotiations happen. Identify any biases or challenges and create a compensation policy that you

then share with candidates. Remember it's not just about salary, but about bonuses, equity, title, and growth opportunities.

See also: **Chapter 26:** Pre-judgements and Prejudices

                        Chapter 42: Onboarding: Getting Started Right

                        Chapter 44: Leveraging your Power to improve Diversity, Equity, and Inclusion

Chapter 42.
Onboarding: Getting Started Right

Once you have a fantastic new hire, get them incorporated into the company culture of diversity, equity, and inclusion right away! Onboarding really sets the tone for how the person sees the company and feels about working at the company.

1. **Review your current onboarding process with some current employees for what messages are being sent to new hires about diversity, equity, and inclusion.** Identify how onboarding groups of new hires are assembled, how the company's values are communicated, who onboarding staff are, how onboarding staff communicate with new hires, and whether these messages are conveying the company's commitment to diversity, equity, and inclusion. At large companies, it's common to have the employee spend the first week or so learning about the company, and diversity, equity, and inclusion should be a part of this.

2. **The onboarding process should include a diversity, equity, and inclusion session as well as information on diversity, equity, and inclusion throughout all onboarding.** This session should include clarifying the company's policies and practices on diversity, equity, and inclusion. Define exactly what the company is committed to and what expectations are from all new employees regarding working together. Share the company's "big picture" or roadmap for what kind of company it wants to be, so new hires can see what the company is moving toward.

3. **Ensure individuals presenting onboarding sessions are properly trained to be diversity leaders and focus on inclusiveness.** Make sure they know the importance of

diversity, equity, and inclusion and the company's goals on these topics. Ensure presenters communicate effectively both verbally and nonverbally and that they are able to be culturally appropriate in encouraging inclusion.

4. **Coach the existing managers and team members to be inclusive to new hires.** This can include addressing different communication styles, engaging in coaching with all employees, and encouraging regular feedback. Ensure new teams are prepared to welcome a new hire, including who they report to, who their colleagues are, where they sit, and clear roles and responsibilities within team. You can always give them this book!

5. **Help new hires learn the company lingo.** Most companies have an organizational chart, but that doesn't necessarily reflect who really has power. Similarly, a glossary of company terms, an introduction to offices or individuals that can be helpful in case of any problems, and some guidelines for appropriate ways to address conflict can emphasize the company's culture for finding solutions and ensuring staff at all levels are supported.

6. **Help new hires get to know people.** Group onboarding can help new hires get to know others in their cohort and on their team. Assigning buddies to new hires can help them get settled the first few weeks. It's also helpful for leaders and colleagues to meet new hires in one-on-one or small group lunches to hear how work is going and to nip problems in the bud.

7. **Provide information in multiple formats.** Onboarding at a new company can be overwhelming! People take in information in different ways, so having it presented verbally, in writing, and then followed up on after 4-6 weeks can be useful in ensuring new hires understand what they need to.

8. **Ask for feedback on the onboarding process.** Check in with employees after a few weeks and months once they are getting settled to solicit feedback on the process of onboarding. What went too fast? Too slow? What could have been more helpful

to them? How can HR help more? How can their supervisors or colleagues help them get settled? What could be improved? Make sure to review and implement feedback to continue to improve the onboarding process.

See also: **Chapter 26:** Pre-judgements and Prejudices

Chapter 38: Building the Multicultural Workplace

Chapter 44: Leveraging your Power to improve Diversity, Equity, and Inclusion

Chapter 43.
Performance Reviews: Managing the Myth of Meritocracy

In the U.S., there is strong belief in meritocracy, which is the idea individuals with more skills, education, talent, and hard work reap greater benefits than those without. Although Americans tend to disdain alternatives to meritocracy, such as hereditary aristocracy (where one's opportunities in life are directly attributable to the family one was born into) many of us do not realize that meritocracy is a myth. Many people with skills, education, talent, and hard work are passed over, unseen, or unrecognized because of diversity factors including race, gender, and age. Further, nepotism (providing favoritism, including jobs, to relatives) is alive and well. Believing the world is a meritocracy makes people more likely to be selfish, less self-critical and even more prone to acting in discriminatory ways.

1. **Understand that companies, the U.S., and the world are not meritocracies.** Although they may claim to promote people and ideas based on merit, there are still too many underlying factors for this to be realized fairly. Also understand that believing the context is a meritocracy leads people to *think* they are fair, when they are actually more likely to be unfair. For example, women and race/ethnic minority men in the same jobs, with the same performance review, receive lower salary increases than white men. That is not meritocracy.

2. **The idea that the world is not a meritocracy is threatening to those who have achieved much.** They view themselves as having achieved their lofty accomplishments because they had more skills, education, talent, or hard work than others. The

assumption that circumstances beyond their control, such as race or family connections, contributed substantially to their success can be insulting. Tread carefully.

3. **Performance reviews are stressful endeavors for both supervisors and staff.** Ensure all staff know what the expectations are, what success looks like, and whether raises or bonuses are riding on the performance review. Evaluate people only on factors they can control; organizations should take responsibility for the factors that are out of the staff's control. Whether someone has competitive/supportive colleagues, a capable/not as capable boss, sufficient/insufficient opportunity for visibility and plum assignments should be taken into account in performance reviews. This will also help mute the myth of meritocracy by specifically calling out specific factors not in the person's control.

4. **Performance reviews should never be a surprise.** Ideally, managers and supervisors are providing feedback throughout the entire performance period. If you're waiting until the performance review to give critical feedback, you're too late. Have the difficult conversation, provide support or training, and help the employee be successful as soon as you see a problem, not once a year.

5. **Encourage all staff and managers to give and receive feedback.** If the goal is to increase individual and team performance, all staff should feel free to offer feedback and suggestions, and all staff should be able to manage receiving feedback. Provide training if necessary so this process stays successful and positive. Reward individuals who provide helpful and respectful feedback – and those who accept feedback professionally and use it to improve their work.

6. **Encourage self-evaluation.** Some employees feel insulted if they are asked to provide a written self-evaluation, but this strategy is helpful for supervisors to learn where expectations or perspectives of performance may differ. Explaining the

self-evaluation as a critical professional development skill can make this into a better learning opportunity.

7. **Strive for fairness and equity in performance reviews.** Incorporate best practices for fair performance reviews, including ensuring expectations are clear, working collaboratively with the staff to get an accurate perception of performance and challenges beyond their control, addressing each criterion, providing positive feedback as well as areas to improve, and giving overall direction to the staff.

See also: **Chapter 11:** Equality vs. Equity

Chapter 27: Intentional Communication

Chapter 44: Leveraging your Power to improve Diversity, Equity, and Inclusion

Chapter 44.
Leveraging your Power to improve Diversity, Equity, and Inclusion

Whatever privilege and power you may have -- as a supervisor or through your personal characteristics – use it for good.

1. **Know yourself, learn your power.** If you haven't already, check out the first few chapters to learn about yourself, your culture, and your people. If you have completed those exercises, go back and review now that you're here and update anything you need to. Identify strengths in your story and in the story of your culture and your people, such as persistence, collegiality, grit, or kindness. What are strengths your people, your culture and you bring to the table? Regardless of the adversity or privilege you and your ancestors experience, you have power. Recognize your power and use it to help others.

2. **Recognize how you – or people who look or act like you – have hurt others or been hurt.** This will help you understand how you can be seen by others. All of us have at some time been unfair or unkind. Many of us have ancestors or parents who have intentionally or unintentionally benefited from and supported an unfair system. You don't have to feel guilty for everything any ancestor did, but recognizing your people's role in others oppression can inspire us to learn better and do better.

3. **Learn about others.** The more you learn about other cultures and ways of being, the more you can recognize the strengths in everyone and in all aspects of their identity. Understanding these strengths – and a lifelong insistence on looking for them in everyone you meet -- will improve your ability to relate to others.

4. **Accept that the system that facilitates privilege and oppression also works against those who try to make**

changes. Although people who are privileged are also affected by the oppressive systems, in the form of fear, defensiveness, and lack of connection, it is often in the interests of the privileged to continue the current system. The dominant groups don't generally view these problems as *their* problems. Further, addressing these issues is challenging because there is fear about what will happen when the systems begin to change. You can work to change minds of individual people – and at the same time work to change the systems that facilitate privilege and oppression.

5. **There is increasing language and space for all people to have these conversations.** As we've stated many times, do your own homework. Learn the language of diversity, equity and inclusion so you can start to name things as they are. This will help you …

6. **… Become a truth-teller.** The more solidly you know who you are, what your culture is, and who your people are, and the more intimately you understand others and the culture and the language, the more you can become a truth-teller who will communicate your observations and recommendations. Truth-tellers operate in the realm of candor, and model exceptionally high standards for equity and fairness. Further, and most important, truth-tellers encourage us to be better.

7. **Recognize the power in others and help them find their own power.** You don't need to become a savior of others to help them find their own power. Once you identify power in others, help them discover what is amazing and powerful about them. Help them see the strength in their culture and their ancestors and the potential for greatness in all of us. This will never be wasted energy.

See also: **Chapter 1:** Who Am I?

Chapter 2: What is My Culture?

Chapter 25: Being an Ally and an Advocate

Chapter 45.
The Courage to Hope

Since you've made it this far, there is hope for our world -- our beautiful, multicultural, multifaceted world made up of diverse, multidimensional, complex, and nuanced individuals. The last few years have seen a resurge in racism, antisemitism, islamophobia, and white supremacy. Actually, the last few years have seen a resurge of hatred. But it's up to you, the reader, to seek and maintain the courage to hope. To hope and dream for a better world is only the first step. Then it's time to act. Acting involves analyzing and improving your world. Our world. It involves appreciating the diverse context in which we exist. Then you align yourself on the side of what is just and right. By not just becoming an ally, but by becoming an advocate for diversity, equity, and inclusion so a transformative narrative can be realized.

1. **Use social media as a platform to highlight others who are different than you or your immediate circle.** Tell stories that highlight your own interactions with others who are different. You do not have to always emphasize their differences. Your interaction will be enough to change the norms.

2. **Read and learn about others who are different than you.** Study their history, worldviews, religions and culture. Do so with an open mind and from a space of cultural relativism—where you place yourself in their narrative—not just their current narrative, their historical narrative.

3. **Seek to interact with others who are different.** After you do your homework, seek to understand others who are different from you. Don't make them do the work by explaining everything to you.

4. **Remember that a diverse team and a multifaceted community are strong and creative forces.** It takes patience

with others, a healthy sense of curiosity of the unknown, amazement with all of creation and the tenacity to stand firm in your convictions that everyone is valuable and should be treated with respect, dignity, and radical love.

5. **Familiarize yourself with websites and groups – both on social media and in-person -- that will enable you to interact with like-minded people who want to be the change that transforms our world.** One such group is called *Be the Bridge*. It is an interracial non-profit organization and community of people who share the common goal of creating healthy dialogue about race and social justice. You can find them on social media.

6. **Check out books and podcasts which emphasize diversity.** Access to most podcasts are free. If you go on Amazon or any other book site, just do a search for diversity, race, equity, intersectionality, and more – and check out the *For Further Reading* section at the end of this book. It is easy to find an abundance of reading materials. Just make sure that you closely examine the description and intent. Some material is written with the intent to divide rather than unify.

See also: **Chapter 30:** Building Belonging

Chapter 32: Communicating for Change

Chapter 44: Leveraging your Power to improve Diversity, Equity, and Inclusion

Glossary

Ableism: The belief that disabled individuals are inferior to non-disabled individuals, leading to discrimination toward and oppression of individuals with disabilities and physical differences.

Acculturation: The general phenomenon of persons learning the nuances of or being initiated into a culture. It may also carry a negative connotation when referring to the attempt by dominant cultural groups to acculturate members of other cultural groups into the dominant culture in an assimilation fashion.

Adultism: Prejudiced thoughts and discriminatory actions against young people, in favor of the older person(s).

Advocate: Someone who speaks up for themselves and members of their identity group; e.g. a person who lobbies for equal pay for a specific group.

Ageism/Age Discrimination: Prejudiced thoughts and discriminatory actions based on differences in age; usually that of younger persons against older.

Ally: A person of one social identity group who stands up in support of members of another group. Typically, member of dominant group standing beside member(s) of targeted group; e.g., a man arguing for equal pay for women.

Androgynous: A person whose identity is between the two traditional genders; Someone who reflects an appearance that is both masculine and feminine, or who appears to be neither or both a male and a female.

Antilocution (hate speech). a form of prejudice in which negative verbal remarks against a person, group, or community, are made in a public or private setting and not addressed directly to the target.

Anti-Semitism: The fear or hatred of Jews, Judaism, and related symbols.

Asexuality: Someone with little or no romantic, emotional and/or sexual attraction toward other persons. Asexual could be described as non-sexual, but asexuality is different from celibacy, which is a choice to not engage in sexual behaviors with another person.

Assigned Sex: What a doctor determines to be your physical sex birth based on the appearance of one's primary sex characteristics.

Assimilation: A process by which outsiders (persons who are others by virtue of cultural heritage, gender, age, religious background, and so forth) are brought into, or made to take on the existing identity of the group into which they are being assimilated. The term has had a negative connotation in recent educational literature, imposing coercion and a failure to recognize and value diversity. It is also understood as a survival technique for individuals or groups.

Bias: Prejudice; an inclination or preference, especially one that interferes with impartial judgment.

Bigotry: An unreasonable or irrational attachment to negative stereotypes and prejudices.

Biphobia: The fear or hatred of homosexuality (and other non-heterosexual identities), and persons perceived to be bisexual.

Bisexual: A romantic, sexual, or/and emotional attraction toward people of all sexes. A person who identifies as bisexual is understood to have attraction to male and female identified persons.

Categorization: The natural intellectual process of grouping and labeling people, things, etc. based on their similarities. Categorization becomes problematic when the groupings become oversimplified and rigid (e.g., stereotypes).

Cisgender: A person who identifies as the gender they were assigned at birth.

Classism: Prejudiced thoughts and discriminatory actions based on a difference in socioeconomic status, income, class; usually by upper classes against lower.

Code switching: The action of changing behaviors, speech, dress, or mannerisms to conform to a different cultural norm depending on context. Everyone does this to some extent, but it is often protective for members of some minority groups to modify their behavior in the workplace, which can lead to feelings of inauthenticity.

Collusion: Willing participation in the discrimination against and/or oppression of one's own group (e.g., a woman who enforces dominant body ideals through her comments and actions).

Colonization: The action or process of settling among and establishing control over the indigenous people of an area. The action of appropriating a place or domain for one's own use.

Color Blind: The belief in treating everyone "equally" by treating everyone the same; based on the presumption that differences are by definition bad or problematic, and therefore best ignored (i.e., "I don't see race").

Colorism: A form of prejudice or discrimination in which people are treated differently based on the social meanings attached to skin color.

Conscious Bias (Explicit Bias): Refers to the attitudes and beliefs we have about a person or group on a conscious level.

Critical Race Theory. A challenge to the dominant discourse on race and racism as they relate to by examining how policy and practice are used to subordinate certain racial and ethnic groups. Critical race theory includes themes of intersectionality, centrality of race and racism, challenge to dominant ideology, commitment to social justice, and centrality of experiential knowledge.

Culture: The pattern of daily life learned consciously and unconsciously by a group of people. These patterns can be seen in language, governing practices, arts, customs, holiday celebrations, food, religion, dating rituals, and clothing. Update definition

Cultural Appropriation: The adoption or theft of icons, rituals, aesthetic standards, and behavior from one culture or subculture by another. It is generally applied when the subject culture is a minority culture or somehow subordinate in social, political, economic, or military status to appropriating culture. This "appropriation" often occurs without any real understanding of why the original culture took part in these activities, often converting culturally significant artifacts, practices, and beliefs into "meaningless" pop-culture or giving them a significance that is completely different/less nuanced than they would originally have had.

Cultural awareness: An understanding of the differences between individuals and people from other countries, cultures, or other backgrounds, especially differences in attitudes and values. Note awareness is not necessarily competence in managing differences effectively.

Cultural competence: The ability to communicate successfully with people of other cultures. Culturally competent individuals understand culture-specific concepts in perception, thinking, feeling, and acting. They also have respect for, interest in, and motivation towards, continued learning about cultures.

Cultural humility involves learning to understand our own perspectives as we learn about theirs, reducing power imbalance, entering into mutual relationships including shared self-disclosure, and working for broader change.

Cultural norms: The standards we live by. Cultural norms are the shared expectations and rules that guide behavior of people within social groups. These norms are learned and reinforced from parents, friends, teachers and others while growing up in a society

Dialogue: Communication that creates and recreates multiple understandings. It is bi-directional, not zero-sum and may or may not end in agreement. It can be emotional and uncomfortable, but is safe, respectful and has greater understanding as its goal.

Disability: A cognitive, developmental, intellectual, mental, physical, sensory impairment that substantially affects a person's life activities and may be present from birth or occur during a person's lifetime.

Discrimination: The denial of justice and fair treatment by both individuals and institutions in many areas, including employment, education, housing, banking, and political rights. Discrimination is an action that can follow prejudiced thinking.

Diversity: The wide variety of shared and different personal and group characteristics among human beings.

Dominant Culture: The cultural values, beliefs, and practices that are assumed to be the most common and influential within a given society.

Ethnicity: A social construct which divides individuals into smaller social groups based on characteristics such as a shared sense of group membership, values, behavioral patterns, language, political and economic interests, history and ancestral geographical base. Examples of different ethnic groups are but not limited to: Haitian, African American/Black, Chinese, Cuban, Irish, Syrian, Cherokee

Ethnocentricity: Considered by some to be an attitude that views one's own culture as superior. Others cast it as "seeing things from the point of view of one's own ethnic group" without the necessary connotation of superiority.

Equality: A state of affairs in which all people within a specific society or isolated group have the same status in certain respects, including civil rights, freedom of speech, property rights and equal access to certain social goods and services.

Equity: Equity takes into consideration the fact that the social identifiers (race, gender, socioeconomic status, etc.) do, in fact, affect equality. In an equitable environment, an individual or a group would be given what was needed to give them equal advantage. This would not necessarily be equal to what others were receiving. Equity ensures that everyone has the resources they need to succeed.

Feminism: The advocacy of women's rights on the ground of the equality of the sexes.

First Nation People: Individuals who identify as those who were the first people to live on the Western Hemisphere continent. People also identified as Native Americans.

Gay: A person who is emotionally, romantically or sexually attracted to members of the same gender.

Gender: Socially constructed concepts of masculinity and femininity; the "appropriate" qualities accompanying biological sex.

Gender Expression: External manifestations of gender, expressed through a person's name, pronouns, clothing, hairstyle, behavior, voice, and/or body characteristics.

Gender Identity: Your internal sense of self regarding your gender; how you relate to your gender.

Generations: Generations are a way of describing individuals who were born and grew up in a certain segment of time with the assumption that because of their shared social experiences they will have similar values and approaches. Millennials were born between approximately 1980 and 2000. You followed Generation X (born 1965–1980), who followed the Baby Boomers (born 1946–1964), who followed the Silent Generation, also called Traditionals (born 1922–1945). Coming after Millennials is Generation Z, born in 2000 and later.

Heterosexism: The presumption that everyone is, and should be, heterosexual.

Heterosexuality: An enduring romantic, emotional and/or sexual attraction toward people of the other sex. The term "straight" is commonly used to refer to heterosexual people.

Homophobia: The fear or hatred of homosexuality (*and other non-heterosexual identities*), and persons perceived to be gay or lesbian.

Homosexual: Attracted to members of the same sex.

Identity: The total of the memories, experiences, relationships, and values that create a person's sense of self. Identity is self-defined.

Impostor Syndrome: Refers to individuals' feelings of not being as capable or adequate as others. Common symptoms of the impostor phenomenon include feelings of phoniness, self-doubt, and inability to take credit for one's accomplishments. The literature has shown that such impostor feelings influence a person's self-esteem, professional goal directed-ness, locus of control, mood, and relationships with others.

Inclusion: Authentically bringing traditionally excluded individuals and/or groups into processes, activities, and decision/policy making in a way that shares power.

Inclusive Language: Refers to non-sexist language or language that "includes" all persons in its references. For example, "a writer needs to proofread his work" excludes females due to the masculine reference of the pronoun. Likewise, "a nurse must disinfect her hands" is exclusive of males and stereotypes nurses as females.

In-Group Bias (Favoritism): The tendency for groups to "favor" themselves by rewarding group members economically, socially, psychologically, and emotionally in order to uplift one group over another.

Institutional Racism: It is widely accepted that racism is, by definition, institutional. Institutions have greater power to reward and penalize. They reward by providing career opportunities for some people and foreclosing them for others. They reward as well by the way social goods are distributed, by deciding who receives institutional benefits.

Internalized Homophobia: Among lesbians, gay men, and bisexuals, internalized sexual stigma (also called internalized homophobia) refers to the personal acceptance and endorsement of sexual stigma as part of the individual's value system and self-concept. It is the counterpart to sexual prejudice among heterosexuals.

Internalized Oppression: The process whereby individuals in the target group make oppression internal and personal by coming to believe that the lies, prejudices, and stereotypes about them are true. Members of target groups exhibit internalized oppression when they alter their attitudes, behaviors, speech, and self-confidence to reflect the stereotypes and norms of the dominant group. Internalized oppression can create low self-esteem, self-doubt, and even self-loathing. It can also be projected outward as fear, criticism, and distrust of members of one's target group.

Internalized Racism: When individuals from targeted racial groups internalize racist beliefs about themselves or members of their racial group. Examples include using creams to lighten one's skin, believing that white leaders are inherently more competent, asserting that individuals of color are not as intelligent as white individuals, believing that racial inequality is the result of individuals of color not raising themselves up "by their bootstraps". (*Jackson & Hardiman, 1997*)

Interpersonal communication: The exchange of information, ideas, and feelings between people through verbal or nonverbal means.

Intersectionality: An approach that classifications such as gender, race, class, and others cannot be examined in isolation from one another; they interact and intersect in individuals' lives, in society, in social systems, and are mutually constitutive. Exposing multiple identities can help clarify the ways in which a person can simultaneously experience privilege and oppression.

Intersex: An umbrella term describing people born with reproductive or sexual anatomy and/or chromosome pattern that can't be classified as typically male or female.

Islamophobia: Dislike of or prejudice against Islam or Muslims, especially as a political force.

Lesbian: A woman who is attracted to other women. Also used as an adjective describing such women.

LGBTQIAP+: Acronym encompassing the diverse groups of lesbians, gay, bisexual, transgender, intersex, and asexual and/or corresponding queer alliances/associations. It is a common misconception that the "A" stands for allies/ally. The full acronym is "Lesbian, Gay, Bisexual, Transgender, Queer, Intersex, Asexual, Pansexual ,with all other queer identities that are not encompassed by the letters themselves being represented by the "+".

Mansplaining: When men explain things to women in a condescending or patronizing way.

Marginalized: Excluded, ignored, or relegated to the outer edge of a group/society/community.

Micro-aggressions: Commonplace daily verbal, behavioral, or environmental indignities, whether intentional or unintentional, that communicate hostile, derogatory racial slights. These messages may be sent verbally, ("You speak good English"), non-verbally (clutching one's purse more tightly around people from certain race/ethnicity) or environmentally (symbols like the confederate flag or using Native American mascots). Such communications are usually outside the level of conscious awareness of perpetrators.

Multicultural: This term is used in a variety of ways and is less often defined by its users than terms such as multiculturalism or multicultural education. One common use of the term refers to the raw fact of cultural diversity: "multicultural education … responds to a multicultural population." Another use of the term refers to an ideological awareness of diversity: "[multicultural theorists] have a clear recognition of a pluralistic society." Still others go beyond this and understand multicultural as reflecting a specific ideology of inclusion and openness toward "others." Perhaps the most common use of this term in the literature is in reference simultaneously to a context of cultural pluralism and an ideology of inclusion or "mutual exchange of and respect for diverse cultures." When the term is used to refer to a group of persons *(or an organization or institution)*, it most often refers to the presence of and mutual interaction among diverse persons *(in terms of race, class, gender, and so forth)* of significant representation in the group. In other words, a few African Americans in a predominantly European American congregation would not make the congregation "multicultural." Some, however, do use the term to refer to the mere presence of some non-majority persons somewhere in the designated institution *(or group or society)*, even if there is neither significant interaction nor substantial numerical representation.

Non-Binary/Gender Queer/Gender Variant: Terms used by some people who experience their gender identity and/or gender expression as falling outside the categories of man and woman.

Oppression: Results from the use of institutional power and privilege where one person or group benefits at the expense of another. Oppression is the use of power and the effects of domination.

Pansexual: A term referring to the potential for sexual attractions or romantic love toward people of all gender identities and biological sexes. The concept of pansexuality deliberately rejects the gender binary and derives its origin from the transgender movement.

Passing: The ability of a person to be regarded as a member of an identity group or category different from their own, which may include racial identity, ethnicity, caste, social class, sexual orientation, gender, religion, age and/or disability status.

Persons of Color: A collective term for men and women of Asian, African, Latin and Native American backgrounds; as opposed to the collective "White" for those of European ancestry.

Prejudice: A prejudgment or preconceived opinion, feeling, or belief, usually negative, often based on stereotypes, that includes feelings such as dislike or contempt and is often enacted as discrimination or other negative behavior.

Privilege: Unearned access to resources (social power) only readily available to some individuals as a result of their social group.

Queer: An umbrella term that can refer to anyone who transgresses society's view of gender or sexuality.

Questioning: A term used to refer to an individual who is uncertain of their sexual orientation or identity.

Race: A social construct that artificially divides individuals into distinct groups based on characteristics such as physical appearance (particularly skin color), ancestral heritage, cultural affiliation or history, ethnic classification, and/or the social, economic, and political needs of a society at a given period of time. Scientists agree that there is no biological or genetic basis for racial categories.

Racism: Prejudiced thoughts and discriminatory actions based on a difference in race/ethnicity; usually by white/European descent groups against persons of color. Racism is racial prejudice plus power. It is the intentional or unintentional use of power to isolate, separate and exploit others. The use of power is based on a belief in superior origin, the identity of supposed racial characteristics. Racism confers certain privileges on and defends the dominant group, which in turn, sustains and perpetuates racism.

Religion: A system of beliefs, usually spiritual in nature, and often in terms of a formal, organized denomination.

Safe Space: An environment in which everyone feels comfortable and safe expressing themselves and participating fully, without fear of attack, ridicule or denial of experience.

Sex: Biological classification of male or female (based on genetic or physiological features); as opposed to gender.

Sexism: Prejudiced thoughts and discriminatory actions based on a difference in sex/gender; usually by men against women.

Sexual Orientation: One's natural preference in sexual partners; examples include homosexuality, heterosexuality, or bisexuality. Sexual orientation is not a choice, it is determined by a complex interaction of biological, genetic, and environmental factors.

Social Justice: A broad term for action intended to create genuine equality, fairness, and respect among peoples.

Stereotype: Beliefs and expectations about members of certain groups that present an oversimplified opinion, prejudiced attitude, or uncritical judgment. They are typically negative, are based on little information and are highly generalized.

Tolerance: Acceptance, and open-mindedness to different practices, attitudes, and cultures; does not necessarily mean agreement with the differences.

Toxic Masculinity: Cultural pressures for men to behave in a way that perpetuates domination, aggression, and homophobia.

Transgender/Trans: An umbrella term for people whose gender identity differs from the sex they were assigned at birth. The term transgender is not indicative of gender expression, sexual orientation, physical anatomy, or how one is perceived in daily life.

Transphobia: Fear or hatred of transgender people; transphobia is manifested in a number of ways, including violence, harassment, and discrimination. This phobia can exist in LGB and straight communities.

Unconscious Bias (Implicit Bias): Stereotypes about groups of people that are outside our own conscious awareness. We all have unconscious beliefs about various social and identity groups, and these biases stem from our tendency to organize social worlds by categorizing.

Undocumented: A foreign-born person living in the United States without legal citizenship status.

White Privilege: White privilege means that a person who is white has greater access to resources because they are white. It also means that white ways of thinking and living are seen as the norm against which all people of color are compared. White privilege includes the ability to grow up thinking that race doesn't matter and not having to think daily about one's race.

White Supremacy: White supremacy is a historically based, institutionally perpetuated system of exploitation and oppression of people of color by white individuals and nations of the European continent for the purpose of maintaining and defending a system of wealth, power and privilege.

Worldview: The perspective through which we view the world; our worldview includes our history, experiences, culture, family history, and other influences.

Xenophobia: Fear or hatred of foreigners or strangers or of their politics or culture.

For Further Reading

Books on Diversity, Equity, and Inclusion (DEI):

1. Winters, Mary-Frances. 2020. *Inclusive Conversations: Fostering Equity, Empathy, and Belonging across Differences.* Berrett-Koehler Publishers, Oakland, CA.
2. Storms, Stephanie L., Sarah K. Donovan, and Theodora P. Williams. 2020. *Breaking Down Silos for Equity, Diversity, and Inclusion (EDI): Teaching and Collaboration across Disciplines.* Rowman & Littlefield Publishers, Lanham, MD.
3. Jana, Tiffany and Michael Baran. 2020. *Subtle Acts of Exclusion: How to Understand, Identify, and Stop Microaggressions.* Berrett-Koehler Publishers, Oakland, CA.
4. Brown, Jennifer. 2017. *Inclusion: Diversity, the New Workplace and the Will to Change.* Jennifer Brown, NYC.
5. Chugh, Dolly. 2018. *The Person You Mean to Be: How Good People Fight Bias.* Harper Business, NYC.
6. Vogl, Charles. 2016. *The Art of Community: Seven Principles for Belonging.* Berrett-Koehler Publishers, Oakland, CA.

Books on Race and Ethnicity in relation to DEI:

1. Kendi, Ibram X. 2019. *How to be An Antiracist.* One World: NYC.
2. DiAngelo, Robin. 2018. *White Fragility: Why It's So Hard for White People to Talk About Racism.* Beacon Press, Boston.
3. Oluo, Ijeoma. 2018. *So You Want to Talk About Race.* Seal Press, CA.
4. Hollins, Caprice and Ilsa Govan. 2015. *Diversity, Equity, and Inclusion: Strategies for Facilitating Conversations on Race.* Rowman & Littlefield Publishers, Lanham, MD.
5. Eberhardt, Jennifer L. 2020. *Biased: Uncovering the Hidden Prejudice That Shapes What We See, Think, and Do.* Penguin Books, NYC.

6. Bonilla-Silva, Eduardo. 2017. *Racism Without Racists: Color-Blind Racism and the Persistence of Racial Inequality in America.* Tantor Audio, Old Saybrook, CT.
7. Alexander, Michelle. 2020. *The New Jim Crow: Mass Incarceration in the Age of Colorblindness.* The New Press, NYC.
8. Degruy, Joy. 2017. *Post Traumatic Slave Syndrome: America's Legacy of Enduring Injury and Healing.* Joy Degruy Publications Inc., Portland.

Books on Gender in relation to DEI:

1. Bohnet, Iris. 2018. *What Works: Gender Equality by Design.* Belknap Press, Cambridge, MA.
2. Jones, Martha S. 2020. Vanguard: *How Black Women Broke Barriers, Won the Vote, and Insisted on Equality for All.* Basic Books, NYC.
3. Gibson, Sarah. 2018. *Gender Diversity and Non-Binary Inclusion in the Workplace.* Jessica Kingsley Publishers, Philadelphia.
4. Tulshyan, Ruchilka. 2016. *The Diversity Advantage: Fixing Gender Inequality In The Workplace.* CreateSpace Independent Publishing Platform, Scotts Valley, CA.
5. Ansary, Nina. 2020. *Anonymous Is a Woman: A Global Chronicle of Gender Inequality.* Revela Press.
6. Airton, Lee. 2019. *Gender: Your Guide: A Gender-Friendly Primer on What to Know, What to Say, and What to Do in the New Gender Culture.* Adams Media, Avon, MA.

Books on Sexual Orientation in relation to DEI:

1. Funk, Mason. 2019. *The Book of Pride: LGBTQ Heroes Who Changed the World.* HarperOne, San Francisco.
2. Badgett, M.V. Lee. 2020. *The Economic Case for LGBT Equality: Why Fair and Equal Treatment Benefits Us All (Queer Action/Queer Ideas).* Beacon Press, Boston.
3. Harrad, Kate. 2018. *Claiming the B in LGBT: Illuminating the Bisexual Narrative.* Thorntree Press, Portland.

4. Hall, David M. 2009. *Allies at Work: Creating a Lesbian, Gay, Bisexual and Transgender Inclusive Work Environment.* Out & Equal Workplace Advocates, Oakland, CA.

5. Molesso, Ashley and Chessie Needham. 2020. *The Gay Agenda: A Modern Queer History & Handbook.* Morrow Gift, NYC.

6. Gelwicks, Andrew. 2020. *The Queer Advantage: Conversations with LGBTQ+ Leaders on the Power of Identity.* Hachette Go, NYC.

Books on Nationality/Immigration status in relation to DEI:

1. Lalami, Laila. 2020. *Conditional Citizens: On Belonging in America.* Pantheon, NYC.

2. Shukla, Nikesh and Chimene Suleyman. 2020. *The Good Immigrant: 26 Writers Reflect on America.* Back Bay Books, NYC.

3. Flores-Gonzalez, Nilda. 2017. *Citizens but Not Americans: Race and Belonging among Latino Millennials.* NYU Press, NYC.

4. MenjAvar, Cecilia, Leisy J. Abrego, and Leah Schmalzbauer. 2016. *Immigrant Families (Immigration and Society).* Polity, Cambridge, MA.

5. Hamilton, Tod G. 2019. *Immigration and the Remaking of Black America.* Russell Sage Foundation, NYC.

6. Nayeri, Dina. 2019. *The Ungrateful Refugee: What Immigrants Never Tell You.* Catapult, NYC.

Books on Disability in relation to DEI:

1. Etmanski, Al. 2020. *The Power of Disability: Ten Lessons for Surviving, Thriving, and Changing the World.* Berrett-Koehler Publishers, Oakland, CA.

2. Shea, Lynne C., Linda Hecker, and Adam R. Lalor. 2019. *From Disability to Diversity: College Success for Students with Learning Disabilities, ADHD, and Autism Spectrum Disorder.* National Resource Center for The First-Year Experience, Columbia, SC.

3. Burnell, Cerrie. 2020. *I Am Not a Label: 34 Artists, Thinkers, Athletes and Activists with Disabilities from Past and Present.* Wide Eyed Editions, London.

4. Pacelli, Lonnie. 2020. *Behind Gold Doors-Seven Steps to Create a Disability Inclusive Organization: An Allegory about Disability Inclusion (The Behind Gold Doors Series).* Pacelli Publishing, Bellevue, WA.

5. Wiggins, Tom. 2020. *Disabled Leadership.* Independently Published.

6. Pettinicchio, David. 2020. *Politics of Empowerment: Disability Rights and the Cycle of American Policy Reform.* Stanford University Press, California.

Books on Religion in relation to DEI:

1. Tisby, Jemar. 2020. *The Color of Compromise: The Truth about the American Church's Complicity in Racism.* Zondervan, Grand Rapids.

2. Horrell, David G. 2020. *Ethnicity and Inclusion: Religion, Race, and Whiteness in Constructions of Jewish and Christian Identities.* Eerdmans, Grand Rapids.

3. Robertson, Brandan J. 2019. *The Gospel of Inclusion: A Christian Case for LGBT+ Inclusion in the Church.* Cascade Books, Eugene.

4. Morrison, Latasha. 2019. *Be the Bridge: Pursuing God's Heart for Racial Reconciliation.* WaterBrook, NYC.

5. McCaulley, Esau. 2020. *Reading While Black: African American Biblical Interpretation as an Exercise in Hope.* IVP Academic, Downers Grove, IL.

6. Colby, Martin. 2020. *The Shift: Surviving and Thriving after Moving from Conservative to Progressive Christianity.* Fortress Press, Philadelphia.

Books on Poverty/Wealth Inequality in relation to DEI:

1. Shapiro, Thomas M. 2017. *Toxic Inequality: How America's Wealth Gap Destroys Mobility, Deepens the Racial Divide, and Threatens Our Future.* Basic Books, NYC.

2. Baradaran, Mehrsa. 2019. *The Color of Money: Black Banks and the Racial Wealth Gap.* Belknap Press: An Imprint of Harvard University Press, Cambridge, MA.
3. Wilkerson, Isabel. 2020. *Caste: The Origins of Our Discontents.* Random House, NYC.
4. Ludwig, Gene. 2020. *The Vanishing American Dream: A Frank Look at the Economic Realities Facing Middle- and Lower-Income Americans.* Disruption Books.
5. Rothstein, Richard. 2018. *The Color of Law: A Forgotten History of How Our Government Segregated America.* Liveright, NYC.
6. Payne, Keith. 2018. *The Broken Ladder: How Inequality Affects the Way We Think, Live, and Die.* Penguin Books, NYC.

Books on Age, Ageism, and Adultism in relation to DEI:

1. Gullette, Margaret Morganroth. 2013. *Agewise: Fighting the New Ageism in America.* University of Chicago Press.
2. Petersen, Anne Helen. 2020. *Can't Even: How Millennials Became the Burnout Generation.* Houghton Mifflin Harcourt. New York.
3. Vidovicová, Lucie. 2021. *Age, Discrimination and Society: Rethinking Ageism Across All Age Groups.* Policy Press, New York.
4. Rocks, Patti Temple. 2019. *I'm Not Done: It's Time to Talk About Ageism in the Workplace.* Lioncrest Publishing, Austin.
5. Applewhite, Ashton. 2020. *This Chair Rocks: A Manifesto Against Ageism.* Celadon Books, NYC.
6. Moskowitz, Bette Ann. 2020. *Finishing Up: On Aging and Ageism.* DIO Press Inc.

Books on making change on DEI in the world:

1. The Arbinger Institute. 2020. *The Anatomy of Peace: Resolving the Heart of Conflict.* Berrett-Koehler Publishers, Oakland, CA.
2. Pulman, Rosalie. 2020. *The Mindful Guide to Conflict Resolution: How to Thoughtfully Handle Difficult Situations, Conversations, and Personalities.* Adams Media, Avon, MA.

3. Terry, Susanne. 2020. *More Justice, More Peace: When Peacemakers Are Advocates (The ACR Practitioner's Guide Series)*. Rowman & Littlefield Publishers, Lanham, MD.
4. Kiner, Mikaela. 2020. *Female Firebrands: Stories and Techniques to Ignite Change, Take Control, and Succeed in the Workplace*. Greenleaf Book Group, Austin.
5. Rockson, Tayo. 2019. *Use Your Difference to Make a Difference: How to Connect and Communicate in a Cross-Cultural World*. Wiley, Hoboken.

Books on making change on DEI as a leader:

1. Catlin, Karen. 2019. *Better Allies: Everyday Actions to Create Inclusive, Engaging Workplaces*. Better Allies Press, San Francisco.
2. Brown, Jennifer. 2019. *How to Be an Inclusive Leader: Your Role in Creating Cultures of Belonging Where Everyone Can Thrive*. Berrett-Koehler Publishers, Oakland, CA.
3. Gassam, Janice. 2020. *Dirty Diversity: A Practical Guide to Foster an Equitable and Inclusive Workplace for All*. Janice Gassam, NYC.
4. Diaz, Monica. 2020. *From INTENT to IMPACT: The 5 Dualities of Diversity and Inclusion*. Networlding Publishing, Chicago.
5. Silverthorn, Michelle. 2020. *Authentic Diversity*. Routledge.
6. Gundling, Ernest and Cheryl Williams. 2019. *Inclusive Leadership: From Awareness to Action*. Independently Published.

Acknowledgements

We would like to thank reviewers: Tanida Mullen, Amanda Brooks, Kelly Farrow, Reginald Madden, Lindsay Harris, and Valerie Weaver. We appreciate Alexandrea Merlo and Diego G. Diaz for cover design and photography, Nick Caya at Word-2-Kindle for publishing support, and Cassandra Blake for exemplary administrative assistance.

About the Authors

Lisa D. Jenkins is a cultural strategist with more than 25 years of experience, including working with Human Resources divisions of Fortune 500 companies. She is currently a faculty member, teaching multicultural studies and cultural diversity for the City University of New York, the largest urban university system in the United States. Her passion spans the arenas of corporate America, academia, faith-based setting, and contexts of civic engagement. Lisa's passion is to increase productivity and mitigate risk by strengthening individuals using The C.U.L.T.U.R.E. Connection to realize cultural competency. Lisa is known for her engaging and transparent style of communication. She can be reached at www.lisadjenkins.org.

Jennifer Wisdom, PhD MPH ABPP, is a former academician who is now an author, consultant, and speaker, and principal of Wisdom Consulting. As a consultant, she helps curious, motivated, and mission-driven professionals to achieve their highest potential by identifying goals and then providing them with the roadmap and guidance to get there. Jennifer is the author of the *Millennials' Guides* series, including *Millennials' Guide to Work, Millennials' Guide to Management & Leadership, Millennials and Generation Z Guide to Voting, Millennials' Guide to Relationships*, and *Millennials' Guide to the Construction Trades*. Jennifer is a licensed clinical psychologist and board-certified business/organizational psychologist. She has worked with complex health care, government, and educational environments for 25 years, including serving in the U.S. military, working with non-profit service delivery programs, and as faculty in higher education. She is an intrepid adventurer based in New York City and Portland, Oregon. She can be reached at www.leadwithwisdom.com.